THE
LORD'S PRAYER
TODAY

THE
LORD'S PRAYER
TODAY

WILLIAM POWELL TUCK

SMYTH&HELWYS
PUBLISHING, INCORPORATED   MACON, GEORGIA

Smyth & Helwys Publishing, Inc.
6316 Peake Road
Macon, Georgia 31210-3960
1-800-747-3016
©2002 by Smyth & Helwys Publishing
All rights reserved.
Printed in the United States of America.

The paper used in this publication meets the
minimum requirements of American National
Standard for Information Sciences—Permanence
of Paper for Printed Library Materials.
ANSI Z39.48–1984. (alk. paper)

Library of Congress Cataloging-in-Publication Data

Tuck, William Powell, 1934–
        The Lord's Prayer Today / William Powell Tuck.
        p.   cm.
        Includes bibliographical references.
        ISBN 1-57312-336-6 (pbk.)
        1. Lord's Prayer.
        I. Title.

        BV230 T83 2002
        226.9'606—dc21

                                        2001057609
                                        CIP

To Wayne Oates,
Who was to me a spiritual teacher, mentor, pastor, and friend

Table of Contents

Preface

Friends and relatives gathered around the grave of a seven-year-old boy and his young mother who had both died tragically. Some read Scriptures, others said comforting words, and then we were all asked to pray together the Lord's Prayer. Hearts heavy with grief, eyes filled with tears, voices thick with sadness, tongues struggling with uncertainty about the right words to say in such a moment, we joined together in the model prayer that Jesus taught his disciples two thousand years ago. The words seemed to convey a calm reassurance to all present.

Few prayers are as familiar as the Lord's Prayer. But has our constant repetition of the words made the richness of the prayer grow dim? Every word and petition is filled with powerful images. Repetition without understanding cannot be adequate. A reflective study of Jesus' model prayer can enable us to understand and follow more clearly the teaching of this prayer.

Our familiarity with the model prayer has sometimes caused us to miss its impact. Prayer is seldom easy. It requires time, discipline, study, reflection, and commitment when genuine spiritual growth is desired. By examining each petition of The Lord's Prayer, I hope we can move beyond a rote recitation of it and explore the depths of its meaning for our daily life. There is no better teacher of prayer than our Lord himself.

Although our Lord never left his disciples anything in written form, this prayer was written indelibly on their minds. Jesus was seeking to give his disciples guidance in avoiding mechanical, ritualistic, ostentatious, and meaningless repetition when they prayed. His short, simple phrases move us to focus on the divine presence of God as we converse with God and to be reminded of our dependence on God and our responsibility to others. Jan Lochman has reminded us that "the arc of the prayer spans the whole of cosmic reality with its heights and its depths."[1]

We often see prayer as an escape from responsibility and service and a call to private reflection. The Lord's Prayer compels us to remember others as we seek to draw near to God. This prayer cannot be exhausted by study or repetition. Its message is timeless and as modern as our latest technological advances. In these pages I invite the reader to take a spiritual journey down the pathway of The Lord's Prayer that I believe will lead to a deeper commitment to the Lord of this prayer and a greater awareness of the rich meaning of what it means to pray. Karl Barth, one of the great theologians of the twentieth century, has reminded us that "the first and basic act of theological work is *prayer*."[2]

I want to thank Carolyn Stice, my secretary for ten years, for typing these pages through several drafts. She was always not only efficient but also gracious in her praise and encouragement. Special thanks is also extended to Daphne Fletcher, my present secretary, for all her work in getting this manuscript completed for publication. My gratitude also to the congregations I have served and with whom I have been privileged to share my thoughts on The Lord's Prayer.

NOTES

[1] Jan Milic Lochman, *The Lord's Prayer* (Grand Rapids MI: William B. Eerdman's Publishing Co., 1990), 147.

[2] Karl Barth, *Evangelical Theology: An Introduction* (New York: Holt, Rinehart and Winston, 1963), 160.

TEACH US TO PRAY

Luke 11:1, Matthew 6:7–13

The disciples' request of Jesus, "Lord, teach us how to pray," sounds rather strange to us in some ways. Indeed it was strange, because it came from a praying people. His disciples were Jews who had learned how to pray at home, in their synagogues, and at the temple. They were taught all of their lives how to pray. They were even told to pray at certain hours of the day—nine o'clock, twelve o'clock, and three o'clock. Being a people surrounded by opportunities to learn how to pray, this desire does seem unusual. Nevertheless, when you and I study the gospels, we find that this was one of the few things that the disciples ever asked of Jesus. They did not ask him, "Lord, teach us how to teach." They did not say, "Lord, teach us how to preach." They did not implore, "Lord, teach us how to do miracles." But they did ask, "Lord, teach us how to pray."

THE IMPORTANCE OF PRAYER TO JESUS

Why do you suppose the disciples made this request of Jesus? I think one of the reasons was that they saw the prayer life of Jesus as an example so compelling that they wanted to know his secret. The gospels record at least seventeen different occasions in which Jesus is seen praying. And there are numerous allusions to other times when he prayed. It was evident to his disciples that prayer was a vital part of Jesus' life, and his disciples wanted to know what that secret was.

PRAYER WAS A REGULAR PRACTICE IN JESUS' LIFE

The disciples also recognized that prayer was a habitual practice of Jesus. Prayer wasn't something that he did only when he was in the mood for it. Prayer wasn't something that Jesus did merely because it was a certain day set aside for praying or it was the right time for it. His prayer life was not like the practice of many of us. For Jesus, prayer was not spasmodic, occasional, or determined by mood, time of the day, or the season. Jesus' disciples saw prayer as a regular practice in his life. The gospels reveal numerous occasions where Jesus got up "a great time before day" to pray. Jesus prayed before the major crises of his life. Sometimes he prayed all night long. He practiced what Elton Trueblood called "disciplined regularity."[1]

JESUS PRAYED IN THE MIDST OF A BUSY SCHEDULE

No one can say that Jesus prayed because he wasn't busy. Jesus was very busy. He was often surrounded by crowds of people, but he sometimes deliberately withdrew from people to pray alone. He sometimes neglected the needs of people to pray. People often clamored to be near him. Jesus affirmed that serving people was important, but he also believed in the importance of prayer.

We sometimes claim that we are too busy to pray. We point to the pressures and demands on our time and attention. We claim that we have so much to do, we just don't have time to pray. Listen to the words from Al Ghazzali, a Muslim mystic: "If you are never alone with God, it is not because you are too busy; it is because you don't care for him, don't like him, and you had better face the facts."[2] If you and I never spend any time with God in prayer, it indicates something about our own religious commitment or more likely the lack of it. Failing to spend any time in prayer says that God is really not very important to us. Oh, if we have an emergency or get in some tight place, then God becomes "real" to us, and we come rushing to meet him. Thomas Merton, in his book *New Seeds of Contemplation*, wrote: "There is no such thing as a kind of prayer in which you do absolutely nothing. If you are doing nothing, you are not praying."[3] Praying is indeed doing something very significant. The disciples watched Jesus and realized that prayer was very important to him.

PRAYER WAS A GUIDING FORCE IN JESUS' LIFE

The disciples also asked Jesus to teach them to pray because they saw that prayer made a difference in his life. His followers observed that the prayer life of their Lord gave him power that they did not have. They knew that he prayed before his period of temptations in the wilderness. They saw him pray before his miracles. They heard him pray before the raising of Lazarus. He prayed before he selected his twelve disciples. He prayed before he made his last journey to Jerusalem. He lifted his voice in prayer in Gethsemane, and he even died praying. The disciples recognized that prayer made the life of Jesus different.

On the Mount of Transfiguration, the disciples witnessed the face of our Lord shining brightly. They knew that there was something radically different in his life because of his communion with God. When Jesus came down from his mountaintop experience, he discovered that his disciples had been unable to heal a young boy suffering from epilepsy. Jesus responded to their inquiry of why they had failed by saying: "This kind cannot be driven out by anything but prayer" (Mark 9:29). It was a secret for which they longed. They had seen prayers answered in his life. Karl Barth, the noted German theologian, once wrote:

> Let us approach the subject [of prayer] from the given fact that God answers. He is not deaf; he listens; more than that he acts. He does not act in the same way whether we pray or not. Prayer exerts an influence upon God's action, even upon his existence. This is what the word "answer" means.[4]

Jesus was strengthened and fortified within through prayer. He was different because he prayed.

THE NATURALNESS OF PRAYER

The disciples also observed that prayer was natural for Jesus. Harry Emerson Fosdick expressed it this way, "The master prayed as naturally as a child breathes."[5] Prayer was a normal occurrence for him. It was not merely an addendum tacked on to his life. Prayer was a vital part of his inner being. It was just as natural as air for breathing, as light for seeing, as water for quenching our thirst, and as food for satisfying our hunger. Prayer was not a result of logic or argument for Jesus, but arose out of his personal communion with God. "He prayed without ceasing."

I wrote my doctoral dissertation on the theology of John Baillie. Dr. Baillie, a Scottish theologian, was noted not only for his theological writings, but was recognized for his leadership qualities. In addition to teaching in several other universities, he returned to his native Scotland as Professor of Divinity in Edinburgh University and later was appointed Principal of New College and Dean of the Faculty of Divinity. He was elected Moderator of the General Assembly of the Church of Scotland, and later he was appointed one of the six world Presidents of the World Council of Churches.

A cousin, who wrote a memoir about Baillie's life, observed that his study with its book-lined walls was the place where most remember Baillie the best. There were three basic focal points you noticed as you walked into his study. First, you saw his uncluttered desk by the window. There was also a leather chair in the room where Baillie would sit for long hours reading into the night. But over by the window there was a small prayer-desk. There were numerous versions of the Scriptures and devotional books well worn from use. There, while he was alone, he read, prayed, and worshipped. "And through that daily, faithful discipline of will and mind and soul," his cousin observes, "it became true that the great theologian and Church statesman was first and foremost a man holy and humble of heart."[6] For him, religion was not just a theoretical matter but a personal one. He not only studied about God as a theologian, but he prayed to God as well. Prayer was a natural part of his devotion.

JESUS PERSEVERED IN HIS PRAYING

The disciples noticed another factor in Jesus' praying. Jesus persevered in his praying. Prayer wasn't a momentary affair that Jesus did and then said: "Well, God hasn't answered my request just like I wanted him to, so I won't pray anymore." "Since God hasn't granted my prayer as I want," we sometimes think, "it means he doesn't love me or he is not listening, or he isn't concerned about my need." The gospels sometimes depict Jesus agonizing all night long in prayer. Jesus concludes one of his parables with these summary words: "Ask and you will receive, knock and it will be opened unto you, seek and you will find." The Greek form of these words means, "Keep on asking. Keep on seeking. Keep on knocking." Do not give up. Keep on keeping on in your praying. God expects you to persevere. Occasional or spasmodic prayer is not sufficient.

At St. Matthews Baptist Church in Louisville, Kentucky, we were very fortunate to have had a young woman come through our youth group who made a name for herself in her ability to play the violin. When I heard Kim Nolen in her violin recital and listened to her play in church on other occasions, I often wondered how much time she devoted to her practice. Several years ago she was one of five students from the United States chosen to perform with the Berlin Symphony at the Suzuku conference. In a *Courier Journal* article about Kim Nolen, it was noted that at the early age of four, she practiced an hour-and-a-half each day and loved it. Through her high school years she practiced five hours a day. She had hopes of becoming a concert artist, a chamber music performer, or a teacher. Today she plays with the Cincinnati Orchestra. Kim did not become a great violinist by saying one day, "Well, you know, I think I'll fiddle with the violin a few minutes." She has given and continues to give hours of practice each day.

If a person wants to become a good organist, or an effective singer, or an outstanding athlete, or efficient in some other area, it takes effort. If you and I want to have a meaningful prayer life, we have to be willing to persevere. It will cost time, effort, and thought.

NOTE THE DIFFERENCE IN THE GOSPELS

The disciples said: "Lord, teach us how to pray." "After this manner pray," Jesus replied. Only Matthew and Luke recorded the Model Prayer of our Lord. Matthew's version of this prayer is a little longer than the rendering in Luke. Matthew has five pairs of lines in his form of the prayer.

Our Father who art in heaven,
Hallowed be thy name.
Thy kingdom come,
Thy will be done,
On earth as it in heaven.
Our (daily) bread
Give us this day;
And forgive us our debts,
As we also have forgiven our debtors;
And lead us not into temptation,
But deliver us from [the] evil [one]. (Matt 6:9-13)

Luke's version is slightly briefer.

Father, [There's no "our"—just Father]
Hallowed be thy name,
Thy kingdom come,
Our bread give us each day,
Forgive us our sins,
For we ourselves forgive everyone who
is indebted to us,
And lead us not into temptation. (Luke 11:2-4)

These two accounts are not exactly the same. But many of the sayings of Jesus, as recorded by the gospel writers, show slight differences. There were no tape recorders or stenographers then. The disciples had only their memories on which to rely. The differences affirm their accuracy for me. Two men wrote the prayer down as each remembered it. But the important thing for us is the message in the prayer. E. F. Scott considers Matthew's account to be closer to the original because it is more Hebraic.[7] Eduard Schweizer notes the lack of legalism and the relative freedom that the early Christians used in transmitting the words of Jesus. He believes that the third petition, which Luke omitted, was a later addition by Matthew, based on the "not my will but thine" prayer of Jesus in the garden of Gethsemane.[8]

THE LORD'S PRAYER HAS A UNIVERSAL APPEAL

The Model Prayer is the only prayer that Jesus gave his disciples as an example of how they should pray. For that reason alone we certainly should take it seriously. There is no question that people "pray" it. It is used often in corporate worship services and recited by the whole congregation. Many committed it to memory when they were children. Sometimes individuals pray it privately in personal devotions. On other occasions, it is recited or sung at weddings and repeated at funerals. Vince Lombardi used to have his team recite it before they went on the field to play football. When Eddie Rickenbacker and his men were lost at sea, he would have his men pull their rafts together each night. After repeated prayer requests, they would all pray the Lord's Prayer together.

The Lord's Prayer has a universal appeal that touches the hearts of all people. This prayer has been prayed in great cathedrals and in small country churches. It is a prayer that encircles the world.

THE IMPORTANCE OF BREVITY

Why does this prayer have such a universal appeal? I think one of the reasons for its appeal is its brevity. In English this prayer contains only about seventy-five words, depending on which version of the original prayer one examines. In the Greek version there are even fewer words. In Aramaic, which was the language of the Lord's Prayer when it was originally spoken, the prayer contained still fewer words. This was unusual in the ancient world. Prayers were often noted for their length and numerous repetitions. The Jewish people had set times and places, prescribed forms, and formal petitions. Many of these prayers often contained eighteen petitions. But rather than a lengthy prayer, our Lord taught his disciples a brief prayer. In Ephesus a devotee would often pray for more than three hours outside the Temple of Diana. Their prayers went on endlessly and sometimes they would fall exhausted. Jesus' example points toward brevity in our praying.

THE SIMPLICITY OF THE LORD'S PRAYER

Secondly, notice that the Lord's Prayer is simple. Whether you are a great theologian or a child, you can understand the meaning of this prayer. The words are simple, direct, and childlike. They focus on our basic physical and spiritual needs.

Our theological proneness is often toward complexity rather than simplicity. Suppose Jesus had given us a prayer like this: "Ultimate Reality, mysterious ominous Other—beyond comprehension. Thou who art omnipotent, omniscient, eschatological presence, existentially revealed, ontologically perceived, our hubris has brought us estrangement. Let the manifestation of your soteriology atone us."

If our Lord's prayer had been phrased like this, I don't think it would have had much lasting impact. I did my graduate work in theology and love to study and debate it. But we can sometimes get lost in abstract and obscure phrases. Jesus chose simple words to communicate the truth about the presence of God to us. Let us not take that gospel and bury it in such abstractions that people can neither understand it nor see how its message relates to their lives.

Charles Gore, Bishop of Oxford for many years, told about an experience he had years ago in Calcutta. As he was standing by the tracks waiting for his train, he noticed a religious devotee who was completely naked. He had chains around his feet and hands. He was lying down in the dust with his body extended as far as he could. He would make an impression in the dust with his nose, and then lift himself up, drag his feet to the point where his nose had made its impression. Then he would get down in the dust and stretch out again. He rose up and moved forward a little more. He was likely going to travel hundreds of miles that way until he reached the sacred city of Benares.

Bishop Gore indicated that his first reaction when he saw this man was disgust and contempt. But his first reaction was overtaken with a deeper awareness of humility. This man, Gore observed, "in his belated ignorance of the character of God and of the way to serve Him, was taking a great deal more pains about his devotions than I was in the habit of doing with my better knowledge."[9]

We don't have to get down and wallow in the dust naked and take long pilgrimages to show our devotion to God. Jesus has shown us a better and simpler way by which we can come to the Father. Through him, God's presence was made known to us.

Comprehensive in Its Scope

Another reason I think the Lord's Prayer has touched the lives of so many people is the fact that it is so comprehensive. This prayer offers in summary what Jesus taught his disciples. It is a brief reflection of Jesus' attitude toward God and his conception of man's life and destiny. This prayer also reveals in a distilled form something of his thinking on the central act of worship. The sevenfold petitions fall into two halves. The first three petitions focus on God and God's glory. The second four petitions turn the pointer around and are directed at the needs of all humanity. Jesus begins by directing us to look upward to God. Only after beginning with God as our primary focus does he then direct men and women to express concern for themselves. In the part of the prayer that looks at our human need, Jesus begins with our basic need for bread, then he moves to our spiritual need for forgiveness, and then lastly he asks for strength in meeting our temptations. Jesus directs us to see that our Father, who is the holy God of the universe, loves us, cares for us, and ministers to us. Even in its brevity, this prayer covers a broad perspective of life.

A Revolutionary Prayer

A feature that we may not immediately recognize about the Lord's Prayer is its revolutionary nature. Jesus spoke Aramaic when he taught this prayer to his disciples. Most of the prayers, which the Jews prayed in the synagogue, were in Hebrew. Jesus dared to pray in Aramaic and called God his Father, using the Aramaic word Abba. In a childlike way he spoke the name of God. He broke through the people's religious tradition and formality, which stipulated that prayer had to be done in a certain place, at a certain time, and with certain words. Jesus assures us that we can approach God directly. He offered his disciples a new prayer. Newness rang through his ministry. He came to give us a new birth, a new song, a new commandment, and a new covenant. In this model prayer, the Master teacher offers us a new awareness of what praying really is.

A MODEL FOR HOW TO PRAY

The Lord's Prayer also provides us a guide or model for how to pray. Many persons turn to the use of beads, prayer wheels, yoga, Zen, or other methods to aid in prayer. Our Lord's Prayer provides an order, example, or form for praying. Another reason I find the differences between the prayer in Matthew and the prayer in Luke insignificant is that I don't think Jesus meant for this to be the only way we could pray. It was given to us as a guide. According to Eduard Schweizer, the gospel writers felt that the Lord's Prayer was "an aid to prayer, a guide to be followed without being bound to this or that precise wording."[10] "This is the manner after which you can pray," Jesus told his disciples. "Use this as a guide to develop your own praying." The Lord's Prayer called for, to use Elton Trueblood's phrase, "creative imitation."[11] It was offered to his disciples as an example of prayer. It provides a creative way for you and me to approach God. The Lord's Prayer is a model for us, but is not the only way we can pray to God.

PRAYING IN JESUS' NAME

You may have heard someone say that a prayer will not be answered unless it is prayed "in Jesus' name." Jesus has taught us that if we ask anything in his name he will grant it. Some people have tried to press for a literal use of that phrase. They think that all they have to do is say, in some childish way, "in Jesus' name," and God is supposed to do anything and everything they request. When you and I pray "in Jesus' name," it is to affirm that we want to follow the model that our Lord gave in the Lord's Prayer. To pray "in Jesus' name" is to declare that we want to pray according to his will. Christ is our standard. He is our model and guide. We want our prayers to be in keeping with what he wants for our lives. We long for his will to be done.

THE PRAYER OF THE CHURCH

As you look at this great prayer, remember that Jesus taught it to his disciples. It was neither just an individual prayer nor a prayer to be prayed in public. It is the prayer of the Church. It is the prayer of the disciples of Jesus Christ. The Lord's Prayer is not a universal prayer for everyone, but it is the prayer of Christ's followers—believers. His disciples can and should understand the meaning of this prayer for their lives.

George Macleod was the founder of the Iona Community in Scotland. In one of his radio broadcasts, he concluded with a story about a young man who entered a Catholic cathedral each day at noon to say his prayers. He would come in each day, kneel at the altar for only a moment, and slip away. The priest watched this for several days, and then one day stopped the young man and said, "I see you coming in here each day but you only stay a moment. What do you do?" "Oh, I can only come in during my lunch time," the young man replied. "I have such a short lunch time that I come in and say a brief prayer." "Well, what do you say?" the priest asked. "I pray, 'Jesus, it's Jimmy.' Then I leave." Several months later the priest was called to the home of this young man who lay dying. The priest said that while he was in the room, he had the strange sensation that there was another presence there. As the young man was dying, the priest said he thought he heard a voice say: "Jimmy, it's Jesus."

The Lord's Prayer was not given by our Lord merely for us to recite meaninglessly like parrots. It is a model to remind us of the avenue of closeness we can have with the Father. It provides us an example of God's love toward us, God's concern, and what our love and devotion should be toward God. Learn to pray so that you have the assurance that God knows your name and that *you* know God's name.

NOTES

[1] Elton Trueblood, *The Lord's Prayers* (New York: Harper and Row, 1965), 28.

[2] Cited in Robert J. McCracken, *Questions People Ask* (New York: Harper & Brothers, 1951), 56.

[3] Thomas Merton, *New Seeds of Contemplation* (New York: New Directions Books, 1972), 243.

[4] Karl Barth, *Prayer* (Philadelphia: The Westminster Press, 1953), 21.

[5] Harry Emerson Fosdick, *The Manhood of the Master* (New York: Association Press, 1935), 155.

[6] Isobel M. Forrester, "A Cousin's Memories" in John Baillie, *Christian Devotion* (New York: Charles Scribner's Sons, 1962), 15-16.

[7] E. F. Scott, *The Lord's Prayer* (New York: Charles Scribner's Sons, 1951), 19.

[8] Eduard Schweizer, *The Good News According to Matthew* (Atlanta: John Knox Press, 1975), 147.

[9] Charles Gore, *Prayer and The Lord's Prayer* (New York: Harper and Brothers, 1947), 5-6.

[10] Schweizer, 147.

[11] Trueblood, 11f.

OUR HEAVENLY FATHER

Matthew 6:9

The noted English essayist, F. W. H. Myers, was asked what one question, if he could raise only one, he would direct to the "all-wise" legendary Sphinx. He stated that his response would be: "Is the universe friendly?"[1] At times his question is also your question and my question. Is there anything or anyone in the universe, other than humanity, who really cares for us? When we lift our voices in prayer, are we met only by silence? Is there an eternal deafness to our pleas? Is life basically a dead-end street that concludes only in frustration, doubt, skepticism, suffering, and finally death?

WHAT IS GOD LIKE?

If there is some Other in the universe, is that Someone genuinely concerned about me? If there is a God, what is God like? Philosophers and theologians have struggled with that question and concluded with images of the "Unmoved Mover," "the Grand Architect," "the Great Designer," "the First Cause," "Cosmic Consciousness," or "the Ground of Being." But those images do not tell us whether the Force behind the universe is "friendly."

The ancient Greeks had a legend about a god named Prometheus. Prometheus looked down on humankind and had pity on them, because they did not know about fire. He took the secret of fire from the court of the gods and brought it to earth as a gift. Zeus, the father of the gods, was so enraged by this act that he bound Prometheus to a rock in the Adriatic Sea, where he had to suffer from the heat and the cold. During the day a vulture would eat away his liver, but because Prometheus was immortal, his liver would grow back during the night. The next day his suffering would begin all over again. This was his punishment for defying the superior gods. The ancient gods were often depicted as capricious, vengeful, hostile, jealous, and uncaring. If this ancient view is the true image of what God is like, the universe is certainly not friendly.

THE FORCE BEHIND THE UNIVERSE

Our picture or concept of God usually determines how we relate to God and what we think the divine character is like. Many of us even as adults still have very childish notions of God. What is the nature of God's character? Is God a sentimental old father who will do anything, anytime, any place for us? Does it make any difference to God what we do or say? God, of course, is not bound by our view, but our picture of God may indeed bind us.

Our familiarity with the Lord's Prayer sometimes makes it difficult for us to see the lessons that Jesus sought to teach his disciples through the model prayer. We usually have the same difficulty seeing the beauty in a sunrise. Who pays any attention to a sunrise? We have seen it before, so what's so glorious about it? Familiarity often breeds contempt. Having heard, seen, and read the words of the Lord's Prayer so many times, we simply cannot hear, will not hear, or do not hear what it said or can say to us now.

THE DIVINE FATHER

The Lord's Prayer was a giant step in communication. Turn with me now to the words of Jesus to see if we can discover something about the nature of the universe and the force that lies behind it. Thomas Wolfe, the American playwright, wrote these lines in one of his private journals: "The deepest search of life, it seems to me, the thing that in one way or another is central to all living, is man's search for a Father. Not merely the father of his flesh; not merely the father of his lost youth, but the image of a strength and wisdom external to his need and superior to his hunger, to which the belief and power of his own life could be united."[2] Is there a force behind the universe that we can call Father, and is the Power or Presence friendly to us?

The Lord's Prayer offers us some guidance here. Jesus told his disciples, "When you pray say, 'Our Father.'" Although Jesus breathed into the image a breath of new meaning and content, he was not the first to call God "Father." The ancient Greeks depicted Zeus as the father of the gods, while Roman mythology ranked Jupiter as the father of all the gods. Divine fatherhood in mythology is merely the name for the god of the highest rank in a chain of other gods. In the Old Testament there is also a usage of the Father image of God. The nation Israel is usually depicted as the elected child of God the Father. God is Father to Israel because God has adopted them as children. God has made a special covenant with Israel. God's act of adoption demands an obedient response from the people. Only those who are obedient to God are seen as true children. (See Exod 4:22; Ps 103:13; Mal 1:6).

The word "Father" was constantly on the lips of Jesus. The gospels record 170 occasions where Jesus referred to God as Father. In the Gospel of Mark it is used only four times, 14 times in Luke, 42 in Matthew, and 109 in the Gospel of John.[3] Jeremias and Kittel, noted New Testament scholars, state that Jesus' use of the word "Father" as "Abba" was completely new in religious speech.[4]

As a lad of twelve, Jesus told his parents, who came seeking him in Jerusalem when they thought he was lost, that they should not have been surprised that he was in his Father's house (Luke 2:49). When the seventy returned from their successful mission, he prayed: "I thank you, O Father, Lord of heaven and earth" (Luke 10:21). In John 17, Jesus addressed God as "Father," "Holy Father," and "O Righteous Father." "My Father is working still, and I am working" (John 5:17). "All things have been delivered to me by my Father" (John 21:15). "My Father, if it be possible, let this cup pass from me" (Matt 26:42). "Father, forgive them; for they know not what they do"(Luke 23:34). On the cross he prayed, "Father, into thy hands I commit my spirit" (Luke 23:46). Jesus had not hesitated to address God as Father. Jesus' use of the word "Father," I believe, indicates something special for his disciples and for us.

AN INTIMATE RELATIONSHIP

Jesus' use of "Our Father" indicates that persons can have an intimate relationship with God. Out of his personal, intimate fellowship with God, Jesus could speak of God as Father. Jesus revealed that this intimate relationship is available to all his disciples. God is close and personable. Jesus dared to use the phrase "Abba" when he prayed to God. The gospel writers did not translate the word from Aramaic into the Greek. It is a word that is so untranslatable that the early church has preserved the original Aramaic word, "Abba." The word might literally be translated as "daddy" or "da-da" in our contemporary speech. "Abba" is a very childlike expression of God. Jesus' use of this word indicates that he spoke to his Father in the most familiar manner possible. This reveals an absolute and tender intimacy with God the Father.

But note the reminder from T. W. Manson, the English New Testament scholar. He observes that Jesus rarely spoke in public of God as Father, because he considered the fatherhead of God so sacred that it was reserved for his disciples who could understand.[5] God is not the Father of all persons in general, but of those who are trustful and obedient.

How would you respond if I had begun my prayer by saying, "Dear Daddy," or "da-da?" You would probably think that sounded too familiar to be used in addressing God. Yet Jesus dared to use it as an example of how we should begin our prayer to God. We, too, can approach God in an intimate way. Intimacy is not the same as sentimentality, however. Our prayers border on the sentimental as we fill them with expressions like "Precious Lord" or "in Jesus' precious name." The emphasis from Jesus is not so much on the "preciousness" of God as his nearness and availability to us.

The word "Abba" is not used to sentimentalize our understanding of God. Jesus does not attempt to make God into some sentimental kind of personality and remove our sense of awe and reverence. The next line shows us that this is not the case. God is not to be viewed the way a Hollywood starlet once viewed God when she said that "God was a living doll." Our sentimental adjectives often make a caricature of the nature of God. I believe that Jesus' use of "Abba" denotes that we can pray directly to God who is always near us. God is available and will respond. There is an old rabbinical saying that illuminates this truth. "An idol is near yet far. God is far yet near."[6] Our Father in heaven, Jesus has revealed, is always near and available to us.

A GOD WHO CARES

Jesus' "Our Father," I think, has disclosed something even deeper about the nature of God. We all long to know if there is a God who cares and loves us. Life teaches us clearly the powerful emotion of caring. The ability to care is reflected in various ways in our society. Our Christmas, birthday, or graduation cards suggest an attitude of concern with the slogan often printed on the back: "When you care enough to send the very best." As we drive down the road, we sometimes pass a sign that gives a word of caution, "Pass with care." Our concern for the underprivileged and homeless in some foreign countries is depicted in our sending CARE packages. We sometimes mail a package with the instructions to the post office to stamp it with a label that reads, "Handle with care." One of the slang expressions, "I couldn't care less," indicates the absence of concern or our frustration or apathy.

If you believed that God didn't care about you, think how that would demoralize you and likely affect your attitude toward yourself and others. But that is not the message of the New Testament. The central message revealed through the Incarnation is that God cares for and loves men and women. The biblical word is that God could not care more! "For God so loved the world that he gave his only begotten son" (John 3:16).

God has been disclosed through Jesus Christ as the loving Father whose love is unlimited. Some of the parables of Jesus reveal this supremely. The parable of the Prodigal Son tells the story of a son who wandered off and wasted his share of his father's money in riotous living. When he came home, his father was standing at the gate looking longingly down the road for the son. The father gave his son freedom, but when he came back there was great rejoicing at home. The parables of the lost sheep and the lost coin reveal a God who cares so much for his lost children that he actively seeks them out wherever they are. These two parables and the parable of the prodigal son are word pictures that express the deep compassion and eternal vigil of God (Luke 15:1-32). God is a seeking God whose quest is continuous because every person is precious to God (Mark 2:17; Matt 18:11). Whether men and women are lost by their own choice, by the fault or carelessness of others, or through sheer neglect, God is concerned for every life, and his seeking love calls us into intimate fellowship. The Incarnation reveals to us that God does not remain coolly detached from the world, but God was personally involved in the world through Christ. "God was in Christ" (2 Cor 5:19). "And the Word was made flesh, and dwelt among us" (John 1:14).

Through Jesus, people were able to see what God was like. We know that God is like his Son, Jesus Christ, who was kind, loving, merciful, and caring. We see this in the compassion of Jesus where he reached out to the poor, the needy, the blind, the deaf, the lame, and the sick. God, to the Christian, is not a "first cause" or an "unknown force" behind the universe, but is the Father of Jesus Christ. Through the Son, the Father has been focused so all could see his nature of love and concern. In the life, teachings, ministry, death, and resurrection of Christ, we have seen the eternal love in action. "He that hath seen me hath seen the Father" (John 14:9).

JOINED WITH OTHERS AS WE PRAY

Notice Jesus' use of "our" Father. There is no "I," "me," "my," or "mine" mentioned in this prayer. The "our" reminds us that our prayer to God cannot focus only on our personal, selfish concerns. We are challenged to pray: "Give us," "deliver us." There is often too much "I-ness" instead of "we-ness" in our public prayers today. When we pray, we are reminded of our corporateness. We all have personal concerns that we voice in private to God. But even then we are reminded not to lose our vision of others and their needs as we pray. Our public prayers are always voiced with our hands united with others. This is not a private prayer that I pray as an isolated "I," but one in which I am joined with others, so I pray "we." A poem by an unknown writer has expressed it this way:

You cannot pray the Lord's Prayer
In first person, "I"—
You cannot say the Lord's Prayer
And even once say "My."
Nor can you pray the Lord's Prayer
And not pray for another,
For as you ask for "daily bread,"
You must include your brother.
Yes, others are included
In each and every plea;
From the beginning to the end of it,
It doesn't once say "Me."

The "our" reminds us that our prayers are not to be said in isolation, focused principally with selfish intents where we remain unaware of our brothers and sisters who also have needs and concerns. If my eyes and ears are turned inward only and on my own concerns, then I have not understood the model prayer of our Lord effectively. When we consider the needs of others, Roberta C. Bondi reminds us to pray with a sense of being morally superior but,

> I must pray this prayer, therefore, for myself, not only to teach me what to pray for the people with whom I share my life and my world, but to train me in an ever-growing vulnerability and empathy for them as well.[5]

I recently visited some of our church members who are in various stages of illness and pain. Several of them said to me, "Be sure to thank our congregation for their cards and letters, but most importantly for the prayers they say for me." Their awareness that someone else was praying for them while they were suffering, in pain, or grieving was a real source of strength to them. They did not feel alone in their pain but felt a tremendous sense of togetherness through the prayer concern of others. The "our" in "Our Father" reminds us of the support of fellow Christians. Thank God we are not alone!

The "our" in the Lord's Prayer breaks down all barriers when we pray. We are directed to say "our Father," not just "my" father, or "your" father, but "our" Father. The fatherhood of God opens doors to the brotherhood and sisterhood of humanity. "Our" reaches across racial lines so we can meet our brothers and sisters in Christ. "Our" recognizes our oneness in Christ. It is a strong word against isolated individualism. "Our" calls us away from religious egotism and spiritual isolation.

CHILDREN OF GOD

The fatherhood of God carries with it the idea of the children of God. If God is our Father, we are also God's children—sons and daughters. Those who have put their trust in God's name have become children of God (John 1:12-13; Ps 9:10). The Apostle Paul later used the same Aramaic word for God, "Abba," that Jesus used. In Romans 8:15 and Galatians 4:6, Paul wrote that we could address God as Abba because we had become God's child through adoption. "Wherefore, you are no longer a servant, but a son, and if a son, then an heir of God through Christ" (Gal 4:7).

GOD IN HEAVEN

Jesus told his disciples to pray: "Our Father, who art in heaven." Does the phrase "who art in heaven" mean that we are confined to some kind of scientifically unreliable picture of God today? We know that God is not just "up there" in space someplace. After all, we have sent sputniks and persons into space. Space seems endless. To talk of God as "out there" in heaven seems to speak of God as being remote. Well, some people do try to limit God with a perspective like that. But I do not believe that is a correct understanding of what Jesus taught. Jesus is not trying to tell us where God lives. He reminds us of the ancient picture of the gulf between God and his creatures. "As the heavens are higher than the earth, so are my ways higher than your ways, and my thoughts than your thoughts" (Isa 45:9).

Religious practice often called worshippers to look up to God. "Lift up your heads, you gates, lift yourself up, you everlasting doors, that the King of Glory may come in" (Ps 24:7). "I will lift up my eyes to the hills, where shall I find help"(Ps 121:1).

We are reminded in the Scriptures again and again to look up. The symbolic act of looking up reminds us that God is more than we are. There is an "otherness," a transcendent dimension of God. God cannot be confined within us or our world or our thoughts about God. God is not limited by our projections of the divine or by our attempts to control God. God is always more than we think God is. God is both *holy* other and *wholly* other.

THE REIGN OF GOD

What does it mean to pray, "Our Father, who art in heaven?" "Who art in heaven" describes the reign of God. Heaven in the New Testament usage was not only the place where God "lived" but also came to mean God's self. When we sometimes say in a slang way, "heaven help us," what we are really asking is "God help us." The Kingdom of God is another expression of the reign or rule of God. Heaven describes the spiritual realm of God. The teachings of Christ affirm that life is more than just the physical. The fact that we pray attests that there is more to this world than the material. The spiritual dimension, according to the New Testament, is as real as the physical. God continuously works in the physical world to make it more like the spiritual realm. The Apostle Paul, writing to the Corinthian church, noted the transition that the Christians made in the resurrection of the dead. Listen to Paul's words:

> So it is with the resurrection of the dead. What is sown is perishable, what is raised is imperishable.
> It is sown in dishonor, it is raised in glory. It is sown in weakness, it is raised in power.
> It is sown a physical body, it is raised a spiritual body.
> For this perishable nature must put on the imperishable, and this mortal nature must put on immortality.
> When the perishable puts on the imperishable, and the mortal puts on immortality, then shall come to pass the saying that is written: "Death is swallowed up in victory."
> "O death, where is thy victory?
> O death, where is thy sting?" (1 Cor 15:42-44; 53-56)

THE SURROUNDING POWER OF GOD

There is another dimension, imperishable and immortal. In that realm God's reign is full. As we open ourselves to God, God seeks to penetrate our life with the divine presence and grace.

A magnificent picture in my mind of this unseen dimension is the conversation between Elisha and his servant as the Syrian army surrounded them while they slept. The next morning, when the servant awoke and saw the Syrian army around them, he was very frightened. But Elisha said to him, "Fear not my son, for they that are with us are more than they that are with them." Elisha then fell to his knees and prayed: "Lord, open the eyes of this young man that he may see things as they really are." Suddenly his servants eyes were opened and he saw that the mountainsides behind the Syrians were covered with a spiritual host of horses and chariots. The "army" of the Lord was there to strengthen them.

Often when grief, suffering, pain, or temptation crush us, we tend to feel that we are all alone in the universe. Just think what a difference it would make if our eyes could be opened to see the spiritual reality of God's power, presence, and grace that surrounds us in the midst of all our difficulties. "Our Father, who art in heaven" reminds us of the unseen spiritual realm that sustains us during life's struggles and gives us the strength to continue on in life's journey.

G. Studdert Kennedy, an Anglican priest who lived in the early part of this century, recounted his conversion experience, which took place on a moor in England beside the sea. He walked out on the moor in the darkness of night. The vault of the heavens was above him and a million stars looked down upon him. The only sound was the crashing of the waves against the cliffs nearby. Although he was alone in the darkness of that night, he was aware of another presence. He wanted to cry out and ask, "Who goes there?" Years later he had a similar experience as he lay in no man's land on a battlefield in France. Suddenly he saw someone coming toward him, and he wanted to ask: "Who goes there?" But he did not cry out because he did not know whether he would be answered by a friend or with a bullet from an enemy.

Alone on the moor that night, he asked the same question. He didn't know whether his answer would be picked up by the wind, or whether the only sound would be the crashing of the waves. But he decided to risk it. "I made my cry," he said. "'Who goes there?' And I got my answer. I have sometimes doubted it, have never wholly understood it, but it remains. If I lost it I think I would lose my soul. I have been trying to say it ever since, one word—God. I stood that night in the presence of God."[8]

JESUS REVEALS WHAT GOD IS LIKE

Who goes there? All of us ask that question at some time or another. "Is there someone there?" we ask. Jesus was bold to declare, "He that hath seen me, hath seen the Father" (John 14:9). Jesus Christ has made the nature of God known to us. "When we say, 'Our Father,'" Gerhard Ebeling observes, "what happens is no less than that the world receives a different face as we hold fast to the fact that in Jesus the face of the Father looks upon us."[9] Jesus Christ revealed to us what God the Father is like. He has shown us that God is our Father, who has extended divine love, grace, and redemption toward us. We can pray with confidence, "Our Father, Who art in heaven," and know we are heard and loved.

NOTES

[1] Adapted from E.C. Wilm, *The Problem of Religion* (Boston: Pilgrim Press, 1912), 114.

[2] Cited in Pameal Hansford Johnson, *The Art of Thomas Wolfe* (New York: Charles Scribner's Sons, 1963), 153.

[3] Joachim Jeremias, *The Prayers of Jesus* (London: SCM Press, 1976), 29.

[4] "Jeremias," in *Theological Dictionary of the New Testament* (ed. Gerhard Kittel; Grand Rapids MI: Wm. B. Eerdmans Publishing Co., 1964), 1:57.

[5] T. W. Manson, *The Teaching of Jesus* (New York: Cambridge University Press, 1935), 98.

[6] William Barclay, *The Plain Man Looks At the Lord's Prayer* (London: Fontana Books, 1964), 33.

[7] Roberta C. Bondi, *A Place to Pray* (Nashville: Abingdon Press, 1998), 22.

[8] J. Wallace Hamilton, *Who Goes There?* (Westwood NJ: Fleming H. Revell, 1958), 11-12.

[9] Gerhard Ebeling, *On Prayer* (Philadelphia: Fortress Press, 1966), 51.

REVERENCE IS ESSENTIAL

Matthew 6:9

The radio preacher was very precise. "Write in and get your tablecloth. It has already been blessed. All you have to do is spread it on your table, and you will not need to pause to say thanks. That has already been done for you. Send $12.98 and you can get your tablecloth which has already been blessed."

A television reporter recounted an episode that happened in a Catholic cathedral. Vandals came in one night and smashed all of the religious images in the church including the figures of Mary and of Christ on the cross. Then they desecrated the altar itself.

A LOSS OF THE SACRED

What has happened to our sense of sacredness, respect, and holiness? It is difficult to find many today who understand the biblical affirmation of holiness. When I lived in Louisville, Kentucky, I read in the newspapers about several vandalized cemeteries. Gravestones were knocked over. Some gravestones were broken into pieces; others were defaced, and crude remarks were scratched on others. Swastikas, hate symbols, and words of defamation were painted on church buildings in Cumberland County, North Carolina. Someone walked up to the altar in a Catholic Church recently and stole a cross and other sacred items used in worship. A Protestant church had just collected the morning offering. The ushers were met in the vestibule by thieves with guns who robbed them of the offering they had collected. Not too long ago in the Philippine Islands, a Protestant minister was killed in his church by a devotee of a pagan religion as a sacrifice to his god.

What has happened to our sense of sacredness and reverence? Is nothing holy anymore? Rodney Dangerfield observes, "I don't get no respect." But who does? Is there no respect for anyone or anything? The absence of respect is seen everywhere. Visit Grant's Tomb in New York City and look at the way it has been defaced. But you don't have to travel that far. Go to most of our state or federal historical parks and monuments and you will notice that numerous persons have painted or scratched their initials somewhere on those historical grounds. History and tradition mean nothing to them but a place to leave their initials.

WHY THIS LOSS OF THE SACRED?

Why do we seem to have lost any sense of sacredness, respect, or holiness? We could give many reasons, I am sure. I will list a few. One of the reasons is that many have lost their respect for authority. Many hold no respect for persons, places, or things. Others have lost any sense of dependency on God. Worship has become so routine and trivial and many no longer take it seriously. Few today are farmers, fishermen, or hunters and are therefore not close to nature. Those who realize their dependency upon the land, the rivers, and the forest for food usually have a strong sense of their dependence upon God. Others have lost a sense of history. They are ignorant of the way others fought, died, and sacrificed so that we might have a free country and the freedom to worship. They have no sense of history and simply do not care to learn. Still others are too busy, have no sense of need, are caught up in materialism, remain self-centered, or are obsessed with the obscene. I am sure you can add others to your list.

It is frightening to observe that no one or nothing wears a halo anymore. But wait—is that totally true today? Think with me. Is it? A few years ago a parade of people marched by the grave in Memphis, Tennessee, of the noted rock and roll singer, Elvis Presley, where they paused in veneration. The people came for hours to that grave. Many still come today. Our whole nation was brought to its knees in silence when the space shuttle, *Challenger*, blew up several years ago. We all shared in some way in the memorial service held for these persons. Many of you remember watching on TV as hundreds of people marched by the slain body of President Kennedy, and we all watched silently the funeral service that followed. You also remember your reaction to the news that Martin Luther King Jr. had been killed, the funeral services for Princess Diana of England, the murder of the young people in Littleton, Colorado, and certainly the terrorist attacks in the US on September 11, 2001. These moments of tragedy seemed to touch a sacred sense buried deep within us. These unfortunate events remind us that not all respect, not all sense of reverence is gone.

WE ARE ALL TOUCHED BY THE SACRED

But why does reverence have to be conjured up by tragedies like this for us to remember? A noted English theologian, Nathaniel Micklem, penned these lines:

> I suppose that a man who had no reverence for anything or anyone could scarcely be reckoned human. I define the sacred as that which is deemed to be of infinite worth, or to demand an unqualified obligation. That which is sacred is more important than life. To the man of science truth is sacred; he may never compromise with truth; to the artist beauty is sacred; he may never prostitute his art; to the Communist, atheist though he call himself, the obligation to serve what he conceives the coming age of universal felicity has claims upon him beyond his comforts or his life; things or fancied obligations which seem to us worthless and merely silly may be sacred to the savage, his fetish, his taboos, but they are of infinite worth or boundless obligation in his eyes; the claims of goodness, of loyalty, of country and home to us are sacred. There is no agreement among men as to what is sacred, but by the sense of the sacred, few if any are not touched . . . . But nothing is more mysterious about man, nothing more peculiar to him, than his reverence, whatever may evoke it.[1]

We all have to admit that at some point or another we are touched by the sacred. Many different things may evoke it in your life or mine—the birth of a child, the death of a parent, the love of a friend, a sunset or sunrise, the color of a mountainside in the fall of the year, a freshly fallen snow, a Bach chorale, the budding of new life on a tree in spring, bread baking in the oven, the quietness of a church, the laughter of children playing, the sighing of a loved one after an experience of grief, the encouragement of a friend in a time of need. Many times, places, shapes, forms, and persons make our list. Can we honestly ever say that we have no sense of the sacred? I think that the depth of the sacred is much deeper than we want to admit.

HALLOWED BE GOD'S NAME

Six-year-old Bobby was sitting at the dinner table making patterns in his mashed potatoes rather than eating them. He looked up from his plate and asked his parents: "Why don't we call God by his name?" "What do you mean, dear?" his mother asked. Bobby repeated his question, "Why don't we call God by his name?" "I don't understand," said his mother. "Well," Bobby explained, "In church we always say 'Hallowed be thy name,' and we never call him that." That is a good question. How come we do not understand what it means to hallow God's name?

The call to "hallow God's name" is the first petition in the Lord's Prayer. It is interesting to note that the first thing Jesus requested of his disciples was that they get their priorities right. When we pray to God, we must remember into whose presence we enter. We are reminded not to rush in with our own "Christmas list" of needs, desires, and wants. We first remember God's holiness. We remember who God is. We are praying to the Eternal God of the universe.

Think of the way small children run to the door to meet their loved ones who return from a time of being away. If you were the returning loved one, wouldn't you rather be greeted with, "It's good to see you Daddy, Mother, Grandmother," or "Glad that you are home," rather than "What did you bring me"? Jesus reminds us that we are not to rush into God's presence with our requests. First we fall on our knees in awe before the holiness of God. We are called to remember, "Hallowed be thy name."

Translators have rendered the Greek word for "hallowed" in various ways. The oldest translation has been the familiar "hallowed." Wycliffe, Tyndale, the Geneva Bible, the King James Version, the Revised Standard Version, the New English Bible, and others have made this rendering. Others have translated it, "May thy name be kept holy." Still others have rendered it, "Let thy name be 'honored,' 'venerated,' 'reverenced,' or 'sanctified.'" But the basic root idea is the same—the holiness of God. It focuses on the separateness or the otherness of God. God is the holy one.

GOD'S NAME IS TO BE HALLOWED

Notice that *God's name* is to be hallowed. A name to us is primarily an identification tag. But to the ancient Hebrew people a person's name symbolized something about his or her individual personality. Abraham's name means "exalted father." Moses means "drawn out," because he was drawn out of the Nile. Jeremiah's name means "whom Jehovah appoints." Isaiah's name means "Jehovah is salvation." Few persons work at occupations today that their names originally indicated. Most persons named Smith today, for the most part, are not blacksmiths. There are few Millers today who run gristmills. Not all Irenes are peaceful. And we could go on and on to prove our point.

In the Bible a name often characterized the person himself or herself. To know God's name enabled a person to understand something about God's nature and character. When Moses was asked to speak to Pharaoh for God, he asked God what name he should use to say who had sent him. God declared, "Say, 'I am who I am has sent you'"— Yahweh. "Tell them," God said, "'I am who I am (the God who eternally is) has sent you.'" God's name revealed something significant about who God is.

Many have lost an awareness of the holy nature of God. Some have depicted God with less than holy images through such expressions as "the man upstairs," "the sweet daddy," "the bosom buddy," or "Mr. Big." The fundamental act of all religion is the worship of the Holy. We must keep foremost in our minds that God is God. When we approach God, we come in a respectful and reverent manner. As Moses, the shepherd, approached the burning bush, he was told to take off his shoes because he was standing on holy ground (Exod 3:5). Before God would speak to Moses, Moses had to exhibit an attitude of reverence. We should give God the unique regard that God's holy nature demands.

Isaiah had a striking vision of words and the beauty of God's holiness.

> I saw also the Lord sitting upon a throne, high and lifted up, and his train filled the temple. Above it stood the seraphim: each one had six wings, with twain he covered his face, and with twain he covered his feet, and with twain he did fly. And one cried unto another, and said, "Holy, holy, holy, is the Lord of hosts; the whole earth is full of his glory." (Isa 6:1-3)

Isaiah saw God lifted up in all of his majesty and splendor. He was overcome by God's holiness and his glory. Many of the great hymns of worship have been patterned after the sublime worship experience of Isaiah. Believers everywhere lift their voices and sing, "Holy, Holy, Holy, is the Lord of hosts: the whole earth is full of his glory." In God's holiness lies his divine mystery (Isa 45:15).

HOLINESS: GOD'S INNERMOST NATURE

The basic meaning of the term translated as holiness in the Old Testament is the idea of separation. Holiness is the quality in God that distinguishes God from every other form of existence. The holiness of God is the distinguishing factor that sets God apart from humanity, the world, and all the rest of creation (Isa 40:25; 57:15; Hos 11:9; Rev 4:8-11). God is other than we are. We are sinners. Isaiah asked for a hot coal to purge his lips so he might be made clean. As he approached God, he was deeply conscious of his sinfulness.

In the biblical revelation God is not described as "the Holy God" in an abstract sense, but God is always depicted as "the Holy One" who seeks to meet men and women personally (Isa 43:3; 45:11). The holiness of God is not just one of God's divine attributes, but is the essence of the divine inward nature, the source and ground of God's total being. God's holiness is what constitutes God's innermost nature as divine.

GOD ALONE IS HOLY

Not only is God "the Holy One," but God alone is holy. Holiness is God's unique quality that belongs to God because of the divine nature. Confronted by the eternal Author and Creator of all of life, men and women simply declare, "Thou only art holy" (Rev 15:4). Holiness can be attributed to other things only as they derive their holiness from God. Since the basic meaning of the word for "holy" means different or separate, places, objects, and persons are holy only in the sense that they are "holy unto the Lord." A temple is holy in the sense that it is different from other buildings because of its purpose. The Lord's Day or the Sabbath is holy because it is different from the other days in the week. In the Old Testament a priest was considered holy because he was separate from other men and dedicated unto God. When Jesus taught his disciples to pray "Hallowed be thy name," he was declaring that God's name is to be treated differently from every other name (Matt 6:9). God's nature demands an absolute, unique position. Whenever we attribute holiness to an object independent of God, we commit idolatry.

A small boy entered church one Sunday before the rest of his family arrived and began to look under the pews, around the pews, behind the pulpit, and every place he thought a person might be. His mother came in and saw the youngster peering behind the communion table. "Jimmy, Jimmy," she asked. "What are you looking for?" "I'm looking for God," he replied. "If this is his house, why can't I find him here? Is he hiding?"

This child echoes the sentiments of many. Why does God seem to be so remote? We all come to church looking for God. But we can't see God with our visible eyes. God is always other than we are.

THE MYSTERY OF GOD

In all of the biblical images of "the Holy One," the mystery of God's nature is apparent. God is shrouded in mystery. God's holiness reminds us that no one can fully know God's ways or thoughts. God's nature is beyond our understanding. God is incomprehensible and incomparable (1 Cor 2:11; Job 11:3-12; Ps 139:6). No figure, image, description, or word adequately describes God completely (Isa 4:25). A God comprehended is no God. We can never fully understand God. God is always beyond our explanation, beyond our theology, and beyond our images. In divine holiness, God is wholly other. A great chasm separates man and woman from God. Our sin always stands in opposition to the character of God.

As a seminary student, I read Rudolf Otto's book, *The Idea of the Holy*. Listen to his words about the mystery of God.

> The truly "mysterious" object is beyond our apprehension and comprehension, not only because our knowledge has certain irremovable limits, but because in it we come upon something inherently "wholly other," whose kind and character are incommensurable with our own, and before which we there-fore recoil in a wonder that strikes us chill and numb.[2]

We can never fully fathom the mystery and marvel of God. We bow before God in all the divine holiness. We kneel before the "Holy One" and acknowledge that God is exalted, sublime, fearsome, awesome, unique, wonderful, great, mighty, hidden, and revealing (Pss 89:7; 95:3; Isa 33:5; Job 42:3; Exod 33:20). If all this is true, and I believe it is, how do we attempt to hallow God's name?

HALLOW GOD IN OUR THINKING

Let us hallow God's name in our thinking. Someone said that our soul is dyed the color of our thoughts. If we allow God to permeate our thinking, our outlook on life will be different. A devotional mind seeks to think God's thoughts after God. We can fill our mind with profane or evil thoughts, or we can direct our thoughts to remind us of God and God's holiness. Jesus said, "The pure in heart shall see God." We all long to see God. But we never see God with our naked eyes. When Moses sought to see God, he received the response: "You cannot see my face; for there shall no man see me and live" (Exod 33:20). God's hidden nature is derived from his holiness, and no one is able to penetrate the mystery of that presence with his or her own strength. Although no one can approach God, God has chosen to make the divine presence known through creation (Rom 1:19-21) but supremely in Jesus Christ (Eph 2:18; 3:12).

The Scriptures declare that no one can look upon God's holy nature and live. But open your eyes. Look all around you. God can be seen everywhere. God's presence, although we cannot easily sense it, surrounds us in the handiwork of creation. There is no sign on the natural world that reads: "Made by God." Thus, many are blind and deaf to God's presence. They simply cannot see or hear God. As Elizabeth Browning wrote, "Earth is crammed with heaven and every bush is ablaze with God. But only those who have eyes to see take off their shoes." Open your mind, eyes, ears, all of your senses, and you will begin to see God everywhere.

John Burroughs, a noted American naturalist, went to visit one of his neighbors. The neighbor was familiar with his writings and knew all about his love and understanding of birds. As they sat on her front porch, she remarked, "Why is it, Mr. Burroughs, that you have so many birds at your place, but I don't have any birds at all in my yard?" Mr. Burroughs had just been watching the many varieties of birds in the shrubbery and trees around the woman's house. "Madam," he responded, "you will not see birds in your yard until you have birds in your heart."

Before you and I can see God in the natural world, we have to have God's spirit in our heart and mind. Then we will have eyes to see God everywhere. Loren Eiseley, the anthropologist, observed that a naturalist often sees the world only in terms of matter. But if one has eyes to see, he or she can see more. He concluded his book, *The Immense Journey*, with these lines:

> I would say that if "dead" matter has reared up this curious landscape of fiddling crickets, song sparrows, and wondering men, it must be plain even to the most devoted materialist that the matter of which he speaks contains amazing, if not dreadful powers, and may not impossibly be, as Hardy has suggested, "but one mask of many worn by the Great Face behind."[3]

Those of us who have eyes to see will fill our thoughts with the "Face of God" that we see everywhere. Hallow God's name in your thinking.

HALLOW GOD'S NAME IN YOUR SPEECH

Let us hallow God's name in our speech. It is astounding to me how many people abuse God's name with profanity today. In the past, it seemed to me that only a few folks used profanity. But today profanity seems to be a regular part of almost everyone's vocabulary. How many times is God's name linked with "damn"? "You shall not take the name of the Lord your God in vain," the commandment states. I know there is much more involved in that commandment than cursing, but what has happened to our vocabularies? Television, magazines, and movies are filled with obscenities and filthy language. They have set the tone for the speech of many. Profanity is an indication of our poverty of vocabulary.

When Sir Christopher Wren, the famous architect, was building St. Paul 's Cathedral in London, he spoke to the construction workers one day and reminded them that they would not want the name of their wife or mother profaned. He told them that if they wanted to work in that sacred place, he would not permit them to profane the name of God. He posted this sign as a warning.

> Whereas among laborers and others that ungodly custom of swearing is so frequently heard to the dishonor of God and to the contempt of His authority, and to the end that such impiety may be utterly banished with these works which are intended to the service of God and the honor of religion, it is ordered that profane swearing shall be a sufficient crime to discharge any laborer that comes to the call.[4]

In other words, he told them, "If you use God's name in vain while you are working on this Cathedral, you will lose your job." He believed profane speech was unfit behavior in that sacred place. This petition reminds us, "Clean up your speech." Our vocabulary should reflect our relationship with God. The Jewish people thought that

God's name was so holy that they refused to say it. How can we use it so loosely in profanity? What does that reveal about our understanding and relationship to God? Let the holiness of God be heard in our speech.

HALLOW GOD'S NAME IN YOUR LIVING

Let God's name be hallowed in our daily living. Martin Luther was once asked how he thought we could hallow God's name. His answer was, "When our life and doctrine are truly Christian." The way we live is a reflection of our understanding of God. The Scriptures remind us, "Be ye holy; for I am holy" (1 Pet 1:16). You and I have been called to be "saints." Are you a saint? The answer to that question is usually negative. Almost no one would classify himself or herself as a saint. Many, on the other hand, would say that they try to do their best and seek to be honest. They go to church, pray daily, and attempt to live Christian lives. But not for a moment would they claim to be saints. Yet, the New Testament proclaims that all Christians are saints.

The word "Christian" appears only three times in the New Testament, but the word "saint" is used in reference to the Christians in the early churches. The apostle Paul, in writing to the church at Rome states: "To all that be in Rome, beloved of God, called to be saints" (Rom 1:7). Paul addressed his letters to the Corinthians, Colossians, Ephesians, and others to all the "saints" in the churches. These letters were not sent to a select group of particular pious Christians among the churches, but they were meant for everyone in the church who was a Christian.

In fifteen of the twenty-seven New Testament writings, Christians are called saints. All Christians are spoken of as saints, holy men and women. Christians are saints because they are "in Christ," who is the "Holy One of God." The Christian is committed to Christ and called to a life of consecration. In the New Testament the words for "holy" and "saint" are the same. In some passages it is translated from the Greek one way, and in other passages it is translated differently. The Christian has been called to a new life. He or she has been called to be "holy" or to be a "saint."

The reference to Christians as saints does not mean that all Christians are without sin. Paul addressed his letters to "saints," but his readers certainly had their blemishes, weaknesses, sins, and perversions. A saint is not a perfect person free of all sin. A saint is one who is "set apart" and committed to the Christ-like way.

Paul, certainly one of the greatest Christians of the early church, was aware of his own sins. But he stated that "I count not myself to have apprehended: but . . . I press toward the mark for the prize of the high calling of God in Christ Jesus" (Phil 3:13-14). As a saint, Paul had not reached perfection, but he was striving every day to grow more like his Master. He anticipated that the Christians in the Philippian church and all the other churches would be moving toward the same goal.

As Carlyle Marney suggested, Christians are called to live the kind of life in which "God is at our elbow."[5] A small boy prayed the Lord's Prayer this way once: "Our Father, who art in heaven. How did you know my name?" If we are really aware that God knows our name, then our living will reflect that we belong to God. Let your life reflect your vital relationship with the living God of the universe.

HALLOW GOD IN YOUR WORSHIP

Then finally let us hallow God's name in our worship. Hallow God's name in your daily worship as you pray at the beginning or at the end of each day. Privately and personally, you honor God's name by keeping the awareness of the holy God of the universe before you. When we gather in any sacred sanctuary, let us remember into whose presence we have come. A sanctuary is a house of prayer—the place set apart for God. Let us focus our mind and spirit totally on God. Worship is what we do for God, not what God does for us.

St. Augustine has reminded us that everything we do in worship should focus on God. "So oft as it befalls one to be more moved with the voice them with the ditty (song) I confess to have grievously offended: at which time I wish rather not to have heard the music."[6] Nothing should distract our attention from God—not the preacher, choir, organ, or any part of the service. All should call attention to God alone. Donald Hustad has reminded us of the difficulty of preventing worship from degenerating into entertainment. "When we sing sacred words and melodies for purely social or recreational purposes, we tend to jeopardize their holiness in worship."[7]

Let us go to church to adore, reverence, and fall down before God. We come aware of God's holiness, and how far our sins have removed us from God, and how much we need to be transformed to be like God. We remember how Jesus looked around at the moneychangers in the temple and declared with anger in his voice, "This is my Father's house, but you have made it a den of thieves." "You have made it," he asserted. Look at the contrast between what they had "made it" and what was written in the Scriptures for that place of worship to be. "It is written," Jesus declared, "'My house is to be a house of prayer.'" Look what many have "made" of God's house. There is a call to return to reverencing God's house.

THE CULTIVATION OF REVERENCE

Elton Trueblood has written about the need for "the cultivation of reverence." No one is strong enough to go at life alone. We all need the experience of worshipping together. We cannot really serve God if we do not worship God. He has stressed the importance of worship with these words:

> The emphasis upon inner development, when fully considered, turns out to be the most unselfish of enterprises, because as we live for one another, the best we can give is ourselves. A man has made a step toward a genuine maturity when he realizes that, though he ought to perform kind and just acts, the greatest gift he can provide others consists in being a radiant and encouraging person. What we are is more significant, in the long run, than what we do. It is impossible for a man to give what he does not have.[8]

When you and I come before God in genuine worship, our lives will be changed. We are different because of our worship.

Karl Barth, the German theologian, relays a story about a group of Benedictine monks engaged in a vesper service in an Alsace monastery. While they were in the midst of chanting the Magnificat, in the middle of their prayers, a French shell exploded in the nave of the church. The church was filled with smoke, dust, and debris. But when the smoke settled, the monks were still chanting the Magnificat. "I ask you," observed Barth, "whether a Protestant sermon would have been continued?"[9]

How could they stay? Because of their awesome sense of the holiness of God! Worship was not something somebody did for them but something they did for God. Let us fall down before God in praise and awe. Lift up your eyes in wonder at God's mystery. Come and adore God. Let your worship give you a sense of awe that we as human beings can worship the great God of the universe. As Jesus taught in his model prayer, "Let us always remember to make God's name holy."

NOTES

[1] Nathaniel Micklem, *Ultimate Questions* (New York: Abingdon Press, 1955), 53.

[2] Rudolf Otto, *The Idea of the Holy* (New York: Oxford University Press, 1958), 28.

[3] Loren Eiseley, *The Immense Journey* (New York: Vintage Books, 1957), 210.

[4] Cited in Clarence E. Macartney, *Macartney's Illustrations* (New York: Abingdon Press, 1956), 283.

[5] Carlyle Marney, *The Carpenter's Son* (Nashville: Abingdon Press, 1967), 91.

[6] *Source Reading in Music History*, ed. Oliver Strunk, vol. 1 (New York: W. W. Norton, 1965), 74.

[7] Donald P. Hustad, *True Worship: Reclaiming the Wonder and Majesty* (Wheaton IL: Harold Shaw Publisher, 1998), 182.

[8] Elton Trueblood, *The New Man for Our Time* (New York: Harper and Row, 1970), 70.

[9] Karl Barth, *The Word of God and the Word of Man* (New York: Harper & Brothers, 1957), 112-13.

ASKING FOR A REVOLUTION

Matthew 6:10

As Americans, we sometimes forget that much of Germany was devastated by the bombs dropped from our planes and other allied forces during the Second World War. Helmut Thielicke was a German pastor during this time in Stuttgart. Air raids had totally destroyed the center of the city. The church itself had been reduced to ruins. He stood in the choir of the Church of the Hospitallers and delivered a sermon that was part of a series he preached on the Lord's Prayer. His sermon that Sunday focused on the same theme we address here—"Thy Kingdom Come." Listen to his words:

> Isn't there a comfort, a peculiar message in the fact that, after all the conflagrations that have swept through our wounded city a sermon can begin with these words. We shall continue our study of the Lord's Prayer. We don't need to interrupt and search the Bible for texts appropriate for catastrophe. The words of the Lord's Prayer are immediate to every situation of life. The farmer can pray it at the close of the day's work and let it wrap him round with the evening hush of its great tranquillity. The mother can pray it with her children in an air-raid shelter as the cargoes of death fly past overhead. The little child, experiencing the first presentiments of fatherly protection, the aged person, going through the trials and pangs of his last hour, both can say it.
>
> It can be spoken by everybody in every situation, without exception, and we can see this with a special clarity in this hour as we gather together, a little bewildered remnant of the congregation, in the ruins of our venerable church, and begin

quite simply with these words: "We shall continue..." as if nothing had happened at all. For if we take eternity as our measure, what actually has happened? Is God any less the Father than he was before? Do the overwhelming events which have just happened have no place within the Message or are not these events themselves a message in which God sets his seal, in terrors and woes, in destruction and fire, upon what he has always been proclaiming in judgment and grace?

So we continue; the Lord's Prayer encompasses the whole world, and therefore it includes us too in this terrible exceptional situation of life in which we are all involved.[1]

Even in the midst of the destruction of war, Thielicke believed that his church community could simply say during that dreadful time: "Let us continue with our study of the Lord's Prayer." This prayer communicates to persons in the deepest tragedies and circumstances of life. Through the years and through the centuries, Christians have prayed, "Thy kingdom come." This petition has been prayed under the rule of tyrants, dictators, slave owners; it has been voiced under governments of totalitarianism, socialism, communism, and democracy. They have all been able to pray, "Thy kingdom come." Few have realized the revolutionary nature of these words.

THIS PHRASE IS AT THE CENTER OF THE LORD'S PRAYER

A close examination of the Lord's Prayer reveals that the petition, "Thy kingdom come," is at the center of this prayer. All of the other petitions relate to or are based on this one. We can pray that our Father's name be hallowed, because we long for his reign or rule in the world. We pray for our daily bread so we can be nourished to serve in his kingdom. We pray for forgiveness of our sins that we may be cleansed to live in his kingdom. We pray for victory over temptation that we might not fail his kingdom. We pray that his kingdom will be a reality not only in heaven but in this world, and that it will last forever. All of our prayers are without meaning unless we put God's kingdom first in our thoughts and actions.

Some scholars link the two petitions, "Thy kingdom come," and "Thy will be done on earth as it is in heaven." They represent a parallelism in Hebrew literary style. There are many examples in the Old Testament, especially in the Psalms. An example is found in Psalm 117:

Praise the Lord, all nations!
Extol him, all you peoples!

The kingdom of God is the realm where God's will is done on earth as it is in heaven.

THE KINGDOM IS NOT FULLY COME

We pray for God's kingdom to come because we know that his kingdom is not yet fully established. We believe that it has come, but God obviously has not realized his objective for his kingdom in the world. We know that we do not see his kingdom everywhere in the world. His kingdom has not completely come even within the church. And the church cannot be equated with the kingdom of God. The kingdom of God is not just an ideal; it is a reality. Jesus came to announce that the kingdom of God had arrived and invited his followers to become committed subjects to the reign of God. To be subjects to the rule of God means that you and I measure the church and our lives as Christians by eternity. Although God's reign may sometimes seem obscure in the world today, our foremost desire as believers is to serve God.

THE PURPOSE BEHIND OUR PRAYERS

When we pray, "Thy kingdom come," we focus on the basic purpose of the Lord's Prayer. This petition, however, focuses on much more than the purpose of the Lord's Prayer. Isn't this petition the purpose behind all of our praying? Our prayer is to have God's reign dominate our lives. The deepest understanding of prayer is the awareness that we do not pray to get something from God, but to commit our will to God.

CENTRAL IN JESUS' TEACHINGS

"Thy kingdom come" was not only central in the Lord's Prayer, it was at the center of the teachings of Jesus. Jesus began his ministry by going into Galilee and preaching the good news of the kingdom of God (Mark 1:14). He told his disciples to "seek first the kingdom of God" (Matt 6:33). Jesus declared that he was under an obligation to preach the kingdom of God. "I must preach the kingdom of God to other cities also, for therefore am I sent" (Luke 4:34; Mark 1:38). Many of his parables began with the phrase, "The kingdom of God," or the "kingdom of heaven is like...." The gospels show that the terms "kingdom of God" and "kingdom of heaven" were used interchangeably. There was no difference in their meaning. Jesus said that the kingdom of God was like tares sown in a field (Matt 13:24-30); like a sower who went forth to sow (Mark 4:3-25); like a merchant who bought a pearl of great price (Matt 13:45-46); like a mustard seed (Mark 4:30-32); or like a dragnet (Matt 13:47-50). These various parables depict the origin, reception, value, growth, conditions of and hindrances to the kingdom.

Matthew's gospel refers to the kingdom of God more than 49 times, while Luke has 28 references and Mark has 16. It was at the heart of the teachings of Jesus. As Jesus hung on the cross, the thief on a cross near him said, "Lord, remember me when you come into your kingdom." Jesus replied, "This day you will be with me in Paradise." The kingdom of God was central to the teachings of Jesus. If we do not understand the kingdom of God, then we cannot really understand God's teachings. Jesus Christ sought to bring the purpose and reality of the kingdom of God into clear focus in the minds of his followers. He wanted them to know that the reign of God in the hearts of men and women was to be a reality in this world and not just in heaven. His gathered community—the church—was to be a spiritual commonwealth committed to the sovereign rule of God in their lives.

WE DO NOT BUILD THE KINGDOM

We must be careful not to speak about building the kingdom of God. No one builds the kingdom of God. You and I receive it, participate in it, glory in it, witness to others about it. But it is God's kingdom. God is the One who established it. You and I open ourselves to be subjects in it. We can't build it or make it. Frank Stagg, the New Testament scholar, has observed: "At least fourteen different verb forms are employed in the New Testament in reference to the kingdom, but not once does it speak of man as building the kingdom. It is God's alone to give or to establish; it is man's to await, to receive, to enter, and to proclaim."[2] We don't build it. We receive it as God's gift. We participate in it as his servants as we seek to serve as members in that kingdom.

THREE PERSPECTIVES OF THE KINGDOM

In the New Testament the kingdom of God is spoken of in at least three different ways. In some sense the kingdom has existed in the past as we see in the reference in Psalm 145:10-14. God's reign was already understood by the Hebrew people as existing in some sense in the work of Abraham, Isaac, Jacob, and the prophets (Luke 13:8). Jesus spoke about the kingdom not just in the past, but as present. He announced that the kingdom of God had "arrived" (Mark 1:15; Matt 12:18). On other occasions he proclaimed, "Behold, the kingdom of God is 'among you,' or (sometimes translated) 'within you' or 'in the midst of you'" (Luke 17:21). The clear emphasis of all the translations is that the kingdom is already present.

There are other places in the gospels where the kingdom is spoken of as future. The words in the model prayer, "Thy kingdom come," indicate a future perspective as do the words of our Lord, "Seek first the kingdom of God" (Matt 6:33). In some sense the kingdom is past, present, and future (Mark 9:1; Luke 22:18, Acts 1:11, Rev 11:15). The kingdom, then, has come but it has not been fully realized in our world. A time will come in the future when Christ's reign will be consummated.

GOD'S REIGN IN OUR LIVES

God's kingdom works in marvelous ways in the lives of people. Sometimes God's reign comes into a person's life dramatically. At other times, it comes about gradually, almost hidden or in secret. God's kingdom comes in many ways in our lives. There is no one way of understanding how God's presence breaks into a life. We may sense God and be grasped by God in numerous ways. God works in a variety of ways in and through people in the world. "The kingdom is God's reign and his alone," Frank Stagg reminds us. "Yet a part of its mystery is that it is given to those who yield themselves to his claim as absolute and ultimate. Wanting to be king, man is slave. Willing to be slave, he becomes king, but king only as in Christ, God's Anointed, he is made to reign."[3]

You and I discover who we are when we become humble and enter the kingdom of heaven. "Blessed are the poor in spirit for theirs is the kingdom of heaven," Jesus declared. You can't walk into God's kingdom proud and arrogant. You have to fall down on your knees and come in poverty of spirit. You enter his kingdom with the awareness that your redemption is by God's grace and is not the result of your own doing or works.

On another occasion during the World War II, Thielicke stood in the ruins of Stuttgart where the churches lay in ashes. A woman came up to him and asked if he were so and so. She did not recognize him at first because he had on work clothes and not his clerical collar. As he stood amidst the rubble and destruction of war, his thoughts were gloomy. When she approached him, he was standing beside a hole where fifty young persons had lost their lives when a bomb hit the cellar where they were. The woman said to him, "My husband died down there. His place was right under that hole. The clean-up squad was unable to find a trace of him; all that was left was his cap. We were there the last time you preached in the cathedral church. And here before this pit I want to thank you for preparing him for eternity."[4]

The kingdom of God begins here in this world. God's reign begins in this moment, in this life. When we open ourselves to God, God comes into our lives and the kingdom of God can begin now within us. Open yourself to the kingdom. That rule has already begun. You can be a part of it.

THE KINGDOM IS REVOLUTIONARY

A word of caution. The kingdom that Jesus Christ seeks to bring into the world is revolutionary. Oh, I know we don't like that word. It brings to our minds images of tyrants and governments being overthrown. But you need to realize that when Jesus Christ enters your life, he does turn it around. He will overthrow some things in your life. He does bring change, and he will change you. The New Testament is bold to describe the change that takes place in the lives of those who enter the kingdom of God with words like "new birth," "new commandment," "new covenant," and "new song." The change that Jesus' kingdom brings is like the difference salt makes on food, light brings to darkness, leaven gives to dough, or the matching key brings to a locked door. When Jesus Christ comes into a man's or a woman's life, their lives will be different, or they do not really know him.

Be careful when you pray this prayer. When you pray, "thy kingdom come," you ask God to come into your life in a radical way. You pray for a revolution. Christ has given us some radical teachings. "Turn the other cheek," "go the second mile," "blessed are the peacemakers," and "love your neighbor as yourself." You and I cannot keep our prejudices, our arrogance, or even our neat systems. God shatters men and women's perspective on life and gives instead a radically different way of viewing life. William Barclay has expressed it this way:

> Thy Kingdom come—what a petition this is! it is not simply a petition that something will happen to the world of which we as it were will be spectators. It is a prayer that we should accept the will of God; that we should pay the price of that acceptance; that we should cleanse life of all that hinders that acceptance; that we should get to ourselves the things which are the passports to the Kingdom. No man need pray this prayer unless he is prepared to hand himself over to the grace of God in order that that grace may make him a new creature.

This is no prayer for the man who desires to stay the way
he is.[5]

It is radical! It calls us to seek first his kingdom.

THE FOUNDATION OF PRAYING

If the petition, "thy kingdom come," addresses the purpose of praying, the petition, "thy will be done on earth as it is in heaven," speaks
about the foundation of praying. We pray that we ourselves might be
within the will of God, and by being in the will of God, we can be in
his kingdom. We know that God knows best for our lives, and we submit ourselves to his will.

A FATALISTIC APPROACH

Ah, but it is so hard sometimes to understand the will of God, isn't it?
We often hear people say that we are always supposed to accept the
will of God. But they say it with a tone of fatalism. To them, the will
of God is simply a stoic acceptance of whatever happens. "Whatever
will be, will be," they muse. I remember a woman saying to me as her
husband was slowly dying of cancer. "It is the will of God, and I know
I must accept it." Who says it is the will of God?

I can hear another man who stood by the grave of his child. "I
know I have got to accept it. It is the will of God." Who says so? What
kind of theology is it to say that God wills cancer, heart attacks, dis-
ease, evil, suffering, and pain in the lives of people? This fatalistic
approach shows an absence of faith. People who take this approach
accept what they think is the will of God with bitterness and defeat.
Instead of taking a stoic approach, let us be aware that suffering and
pain are a burden to God, and pray that we may share that burden
with God.

A HOSTILE APPROACH

Others speak of accepting the will of God with resentment. "Why did
God do this to me?" they ask. "What have I done to deserve this? I
thought I lived a good life. Why is God doing this to me?" Some bury

the anger they feel toward God deep within them. Some people wrestle all of their lives with feelings of guilt and hostility toward God because they thought his will brought pain, suffering, or grief to them or a loved one.

Reinhold Niebuhr, the renowned American teacher of ethics, asked his young daughter to go for a walk with him one day. She indicated that she really didn't want to go. But he stressed the benefits of fresh air and exercise. In the end she went with him. Later when they got back home from the walk, Niebuhr said to her: "Now aren't you glad that you decided to come?" "I didn't decide," she replied. "You were just bigger!"[6]

Some of us feel that way about God. "I didn't want this decision," we exclaim. "This is not what I want." But because God is "bigger," we feel we have to accept it.

TRYING TO UNDERSTAND GOD'S WILL

We really need to come to a better understanding of God's nature and what kind of world he has created. God does not send evil, suffering, and pain into our lives. God has created a world where the possibility for these trials exists, but God does not deliberately direct them on us as punishment. We could not grow and become full persons without the possibility of pain, suffering, and sin. God doesn't pick out Henry, Nancy, Bill, or Jim and say, "I'm going to give you cancer, etc." What kind of God would that be? *Why* do we attribute to God something so awful that, if a person did it, we would lock him or her in jail for doing it?

We all have to confess that it is not easy to understand God's will. Who hasn't had difficulty discerning the designs of God's way and purpose in their lives? As Christians, we all long to have a clear word. Some of you may have seen Doug Marlette's comic strip about a preacher called Rev. Will B. Dunn. In this comic strip the preacher wears an old-fashioned black suit with a pilgrim-looking hat. One of the strips shows Will taking a hike in the mountains. He has a knapsack on his back. As he walks, he talks with God. "Lord," he says, "I have some doubts. But I'm seriously considering going into politics. So if you disapprove, Lord, just give me a sign." In the next caption,

Will is walking along quietly. Beside him there is a loud rumble and crack. "You know…" Will continues, "like a rainbow, or a dove, or a burning bush . . . whatever." Beside him in bold letters that are probably twenty feet high appear the words, "FORGET IT."[7] But Will B. Dunn doesn't see it. And too often neither do we.

God seeks to speak to us through persons, events, books, the Scriptures, worship, and in so many other ways, but we do not hear. He wants to guide us into doing his will, but we have great difficulty in discerning it. The doorway into discovering his will is humility. We bow down before him and say, "I do not want to put myself as first priority, but I want to know what you would have me do in life."

Dwight L. Moody, the American evangelist, once attended a meeting in Ireland. He heard Henry Varley say, "The world has yet to see what God can do with and through and in a man who is fully and wholly consecrated to him." The next Sunday Moody was in Spurgeon's Tabernacle listening to the powerful preaching of Spurgeon. In that place, Moody quietly prayed, "Well, by the Holy Spirit in me, I will be one of those men!"[8]

GOD'S WILL BE DONE

In humility we place our life before God and pray: "God, I want to open my life that your will may be done in and through me." This prayer is not for some pie-in-the-sky desire that we might have in heaven, but is a prayer to experience God's presence and will here in this world. As Dante said, "In God's will is our peace." God's will is not something awful for your life. It is not something evil, harmful, or destructive. God's will enables us to live life as it was created to be lived. God's will brings inner peace. This doesn't mean that God always leads us into a life free of all difficulties or struggles.

I know you remember reading about our Lord praying in the Garden of Gethsemane. "Oh, God," he prayed, "if it is possible, let this cup pass from me. Nevertheless not what I will, but what you will." This prayer was not a stoic acceptance of the inevitable. It was obedience to his Father. He was seeking to understand God's way, then he was willing to follow him into difficult situations, even to die, if necessary.

Dying on the cross, Jesus cried out to God to answer him in his moment of great need. Barbara Brown Taylor notes that Jesus' prayer is met with silence. She continues:

> In the silence surrounding his death, Jesus became the best possible companion for those whose prayers are not answered, who would give anything just to hear God call them by name. Him too. He wanted that, too, and he did not get it. What he got, instead, was a fathomless silence in which to cry out. Forever after, everyone who had heard him bellow into it has had to wonder: Is that the voice of God?[9]

Sometimes God's answer is given in silence, like the silence of the cross and the empty tomb. Our longing, asking, pleading, and crying may be the vehicle to convey the silent presence of God. The "answer" may be communicated to us as it was to Elijah (1 Kgs 19:12)—in the "sound of silence."

GOD'S REVOLUTIONARY WAY

When God comes into your life, it is revolutionary. God challenges us to live our lives according to his will, his way, and his purpose. Let me mention several persons I know who took their desire to know his will seriously. Several years ago, a young surgeon stood in his Sunday school class and told the group of young adults that he and his family were leaving Louisville to become missionaries in Hong Kong. There he would practice his surgery in the name of Christ. God's will for his life took him across the ocean.

William Stringfellow, a white man, gave up a lucrative law practice to do legal council for blacks and Puerto Ricans in an East Harlem ghetto. He believed that Christ called him to serve him there. Martin Luther King Jr. was offered several university professorships when he received his Ph.D. from Boston University. But he gave up those offers to go serve as pastor of a small church in Alabama. There God worked through his life. Clarence Jordon gave up opportunities to pastor or teach in order to establish a small farm in Georgia—called Koinonia.

Through this experimental Christian community, God touched many lives.

The reign of God may lead us into strange places and difficult circumstances, but in that will we shall discover his peace and the real meaning for life. Real peace comes in our lives when we can pray: "Thy kingdom come, thy will be done on earth as it is in heaven."

A missionary and his young son were visiting a Muslim temple. When it came time for the hour of prayer, the caller went to the wall and announced, "There is but one god and he is Allah. He has but one prophet and he is Mohammed." It echoed around through the chambers. The missionary, unable to restrain himself any longer, cupped his hands to his mouth and shouted: "There is but one God and his son is Jesus Christ, King of Kings, and Lord of Lords. And he shall reign forever and ever and ever." His words echoed through the building. His young son pulled at his father's coat and exclaimed: "Daddy, they just can't stop it, can they?"

NOTES

[1] Helmut Thielicke, *Our Heavenly Father* (New York: Harper & Row, 1960), 55-56.

[2] Frank Stagg, *New Testament Theology* (Nashville: Broadman Press, 1962), 153.

[3] Stagg, 169.

[4] Thielicke, 65-66.

[5] William Barclay, *The Plain Man Looks at the Lord's Prayer* (London: Fontana Books, 1964), 76-77.

[6] June Bingham, *Courage to Change*, (New York: Charles Scribner's Sons, 1961).

[7] Doug Marlette, *There's No Business Like Soul Business* (Atlanta: Peachtree Publishers, 1987).

[8] Henry Albus, *A Treasury of Dwight L. Moody* (Grand Rapids: Wm. B. Eerdmans, 1949), 33-34.

[9] Barbara Brown Taylor, *When God Was Silent* (Cambridge: Cowley Publications, 1998), 78.

Our Daily Bread

Matthew 6:11

Few of us, I expect, have ever been hungry. Oh, we may have had some slight gnawing pains that indicated it was time to eat, but I can say, probably without fear of contradiction, that few persons reading these lines have ever really known hunger. Millions of people around the world today, however, are starving to death at the present time. This is not just a few but millions! In fact, if the persons starving right now could form a single line, they would encircle the earth and cross water and land twenty-five times. Real hunger is a genuine problem for millions of people.

SOME PEOPLE UNDERSTAND HUNGER

When Jesus taught his disciples to pray for daily bread, he spoke to a nation of people who knew hunger. Many of the people of Israel lived at the edge of starvation most of their lives. They could never go down to a convenience store or over to a chain grocery store and buy bread. Most families baked their own bread each day. Many of them ate meat only once a week, if they were lucky enough to get it then.

David H. C. Read, who served as a chaplain during the Second World War, said that one summer evening in 1940 he ate an exquisite meal in a lovely French restaurant in Normandy. But ten days later he was in a prisoner of war camp. The rations of food for each day were issued every evening. The prisoners received one loaf of bread that eight men had to divide. How quickly he was snatched from the lap of luxury and thrust into a new understanding of bread as the staff of life. "'Give us this day our daily bread,' took on a new meaning," he said.[1]

I remember a woman in my congregation in Bristol, Virginia, who had been a prisoner in the German concentration camps during the Nazi regime. On occasion, she spoke about her struggle to find food enough to survive. But this prayer of Jesus is not directed merely at those who are starving. It addresses all of us. Let's see if we can direct the meaning that Jesus is trying to teach in this brief petition.

OUR DEPENDENCE UPON GOD

This petition begins with a reminder of our absolute dependence on God. "Give us our daily bread." Ultimately all that we have comes to us as a gift from God. It doesn't make any difference whether we are rich or poor, educated or uneducated, we are all ultimately dependent on God. The soil and the seeds we plant in that soil are gifts from God. We work the soil to grow crops or fruit, but no one is of independent means. Our work and the soil need the sunshine, the rain, and the passing of the seasons to produce results. After the seed has been planted and nature does its part, the crop from the seed has to be harvested, thrashed, transported to the granary, then to the baker, and finally it is distributed. You and I depend on the earth and all of the elements of nature as well as a host of other people to get our bread.

This petition does not just ask for bread; it reminds us that we are to seek *God's* bread. This petition recognizes the source of our bread. Only God, in the final analysis, can supply our basic needs. This thought is expressed in the following lines:

> Back of the loaf is the snowy flour,
> And back of the flour the meal,
> And back of the meal is the wheat and shower
> And the sun and the Father's will.[2]

ACKNOWLEDGING OUR DEPENDENCE

When we acknowledge our dependence on God, we take a giant step toward affirming God's sovereignty. Humility becomes the doorway that affirms our dependence on God. Our humility pushes us to our knees where we express thanksgiving to the Source from whom all good gifts come (Ps 104:27-28). We affirm, "In the beginning God created . . . " (Gen 1:1). "Every *good* and perfect gift comes from above" (Jas 1:17).

You may have seen the painting of an elderly man who sits at a crudely built table with a bowl of soup and a loaf of bread for his meal. He bows his head in prayer as he expresses thanks for his food. Like this man, we pause in humility to acknowledge God as the origin of all things. He is the giver.

This petition does not mean that we are simply to sit back and fold our hands and pray, "Gimme God," and then wait for God to give us everything we want. The Apostle Paul must have faced this problem with some Christians who thought that they did not need to work, only pray. Paul wrote the Thessalonian church and stated very emphatically: "The man who will not work shall not eat" (2 Thess 3:10). We can't expect God to give us food without cooperating with God through our own labor. This is not a call for folded hands of idleness. Prayer and work go together. This petition acknowledges that there is no food apart from God. Ultimately God is the origin of all you and I have.

A PRAYER OF MODERATION

We can go a step further into the petition and note that it call us to a simplicity of life. We pray for bread. "Give us this day our daily bread." It is a prayer of moderation. We are not to ask for cake or pie but for bread—the necessity of life. Luther insisted that daily bread symbolized the necessities that a person had to have for the support and comfort of existence such as food, shelter, clothing, and the like. This petition does not focus on luxuries.

I heard a television evangelist say that he prayed to God and God gave him a Rolls Royce. Another said God "rewarded" him with a thousand dollars. Their god is not the same God the New Testament declares. Jesus was not encouraging us to pray for luxuries! He reminds us that God is concerned about our having the basic necessities of life. If we pray selfishly for cake when there are so many who do not have bread, we do not really understand the Christian faith.

MODESTY IN OUR PRAYING

This petition reminds us of our need for modesty in our requests before God. The prayer for bread is not a desire for the costly or elaborate. Our request to God cannot be for wealth, fame, prestige, expensive cars, or big houses. This prayer asks for something simple, not extravagant. Jesus said, "one's life does not consist in the abundance of possessions" (Luke 12:15). How much bread is enough? Is there a limit to our material possessions?

CONCERN FOR OUR BASIC NEED

The simple request for bread, however, does acknowledge that God is deeply concerned about our basic physical needs. The gospels record the fact that Jesus fed five thousand when they were hungry in a wilderness place. He reached out to the sick, the blind, the deaf, and the lame. He acknowledged a woman's grief when she lost her son. He noticed a widow at the offering box in the Temple. The problem of hunger and other human needs seemed to be constantly on his mind. Through his ministry and teachings, Jesus affirmed his Father's concern about our basic needs. He assured us that it was all right to bring our hurts, pains, sorrows, and other physical needs to God. Jesus was not embarrassed to acknowledge that our spiritual needs are tied to our physical needs.

ESSENTIAL FOOD FOR SERVICE

This simple request may be instead a prayer for the essential bread for service in his kingdom. Earlier in the prayer we recognized that we are to pray with the awareness of the divine holiness of God's name. We pray that his kingdom will come and that God's will might be done. Now the prayer voices our request that we might have the essential food to sustain us to serve him. "When the kingdom of God determines a man's way of thinking, he also learns to administer and use properly the things God has already given him."[3]

This prayer is not that we sit around and become fat from eating God's bread or receive special recognition, but that we might have the necessary food to serve God in the struggle against evil. The request for bread is modest. It is not a request for a small amount of bread for each day but a request for the food that will be sufficient for serving in the kingdom that Christ has come to initiate. This petition is a summons to action—"Give us enough food to sustain us in your kingdom's work."

AFFIRMING OUR TRUST IN GOD

Move a step further and notice that this petition reminds us that we are to trust God. "Give us *this day* our *daily bread.*" Or as Luke expresses it, "Give us day by day our daily bread." The Greek word, "epiousios," for "daily" has been a storm-center of controversy for New Testament scholars. Literally it means, "belonging to tomorrow." This is the only place in the New Testament where this Greek word for "daily" is used. Scholars have also not located it in any other Greek writings. It is uncertain whether Jesus made up this word or whether the gospel writer coined it. William Barclay notes that this word was discovered on an ancient papyrus fragment that was really a woman's shopping list.[4]

BREAD FOR THE COMING DAY

Jeremias points out that this word appeared in the Aramaic *Gospel of the Nazarenes* as "mahar" which means "tomorrow." He believes that this is most likely the original meaning of the word since Jesus spoke Aramaic, and that this word has been passed down to us in uninterrupted usage from the original Aramaic wording that Jesus used when he taught his disciples. He translates this petition like this, "Our bread for tomorrow give us today."[5] This Aramaic translation of Matthew has been convincing to scholars like Eduard Schweizer.[6] Other scholars have translated it to mean: "daily bread," "the bread of necessity," "the necessary bread," "today's bread," "bread for the coming day," or "dependable bread." The best scholarship seems to fall on the side of the translation, "Give us bread for the coming day."

Childlike Trust

Whatever the basic meaning is, its central focus is a childlike trust. We lean in trust upon God from day to day. We cast our worries and anxieties on God. We trust the One who alone can provide for us. Remember the story in Exodus 16 about Israel's wandering in the wilderness for forty years. They were assured that God would care for them in the desert. God provided manna for them to eat each day. They discovered the small white flakes or droppings, which may have fallen from tamarisk bushes and crystallized when they hit the ground. These honey-like wafers were sufficient for each day. If they tried to store them, they became infested with worms. On the day before the Sabbath, they gathered enough to last two days and they were not infected. This manna was a sign to Israel of their dependence on God and God's care for them.

Jesus reminded his disciples, "Do not worry about tomorrow" (Matt 6:34). Do not be overly concerned with earthly things. Our prayer for bread *this day* indicates our awareness or our dependence ultimately upon God, who provides for our basic needs. Walk by faith in the day you have before you. Trust God. Lean upon God as a child relies upon a parent.

Margaret Lee Runbeck, the author of a play entitled *Hope of Earth*, speaks about trust in the following scene. Amoret is talking slyly to Grandma. "I notice you talk about God as if He was just somebody you know . . . " he remarks, "just a part of your own family." "That's right." Grandma said . . . "Don't make no difference what happens to people if they got hold of God's shirttail. That'll pull 'em through anything."[7]

Some of us have to acknowledge that when we fell into the depths of despondency and struggle to find direction and hope, sometimes all we really felt we had hold of was God's shirttail. But in hanging on to that small bit of God's presence, we were conscious that God was hanging on to us, and God pulled us through.

William Osler, the English physician and essayist, advised his readers to live in day-tight compartments. He reminds us that Christ told a parable about workers who were hired by the day; we are told by our Lord to take no thought for tomorrow; and we are to ask for our daily bread only for this day. His advice is not to let the past nor the future bind us. "It is the practice of living for the day only, and for the day's work . . . . *Our main business is not to see what lies dimly at a distance, but to do what lies clearly at hand.*"[8]

OUR INVOLVEMENT WITH OTHERS

Take another step with me into the meaning of this petition and hear its call to our involvement with others. The Lord's Prayer can never be prayed selfishly. We do not pray, "Give *me*," or "*I* want this," or Meet *my* . . . ." We always pray, "*Our* Father," "Give *us*." "Lead *us*." "Forgive *us*." "Give *us* this day *our* daily bread." When we pray *Our* Father we have to remember others. Our prayer for daily bread reminds us of our brothers and sisters in the world who are hungry. The bread question is the question of all times and countries. We cannot be content that we have bread when there are millions who do not. How can we be content to eat in luxury when there are others starving to death?

Suppose you were eating in a room with others. Could you put all of the food at your end of the table and say to the other hungry people in the room: "I have a lot to eat, but I am not going to share any of it with you"?

THE HUNGRY WORLD

Unfortunately, we are doing that as a nation. We have a great bounty, but we store it and seldom share it. I know there is no simple solution to feeding a hungry world, but you and I are challenged as Christians to find solutions to this problem. More people are hungry in the world today than have ever been. Studies reveal that one person in eight is hungry today. There are 500 million chronically malnourished persons in the world. The shocking fact is that there are twice as many hungry people today as a decade ago. More than 15 million children, mostly in Asia, Africa, and Latin America, die of hunger and related illnesses. We cannot shut our eyes and ears to the sights and signs of malnourished bodies and the wailing cries of pain. Your prayer and my prayer for daily bread is directed to *our* Father, and we ask that he give *us our* daily bread. Our lives are intertwined with our fellow men and women around the world.

Following the death of F. Scott Fitzgerald, a plot for a play that he never completed was discovered among his papers and writings. The plot was simple. Five members of the same family were going to inherit a stately mansion. It would become theirs if they could learn to live together in that one house. Isn't that the story of the life of the human race? We are all fellow citizens on this planet, and we have got to learn to live together with each other or we perish together. Our planet cannot long survive if we continue to live in isolation.

THE BREAD OF LIFE

We cannot think long about our need for physical bread without that bread pointing us to the Bread of Life. In fact, Jeremias, the New Testament scholar, believes that the request for "our bread for tomorrow" directs the Christian toward the ultimate banquet feast where Christ the Messiah will feed all humanity with the "bread of life"— "the heavenly manna." According to Jeremias, the prayer for bread for the coming day refers to "the great tomorrow, the final consummation."[9]

Our prayer for daily physical bread can and should direct us to the Lord's Table. Whenever we break any daily bread, it should remind us of the Bread of Life. Do you remember the story about the two men walking on the road to Emmaus after the resurrection of Jesus? When Jesus overtook them, they did not recognize him. Later when they sat down to eat and Jesus took bread, blessed it, and gave it to them, they recognized him. Luke records the conclusion this way. "He was known to them in the breaking of the bread" (Luke 24:35).

PHYSICAL BREAD POINTS TO THE BREAD

When we break our ordinary daily bread, let it remind us of the One who is the Bread of Life. We can and should pray for our physical needs, but let us always remember to acknowledge that we never live by bread alone. Remember the words of our Lord, "I am the living bread which came down out of heaven; if any man eat of this bread, he shall live for ever: and the bread which I will give is my flesh, for the life of the world" (John 6:51). Jesus said, "I am the Bread of Life: He that cometh to me shall never hunger" (John 6:35). We cry out with the disciples, "Lord, evermore give us this bread" (John 6:34).

You and I have to be fed by the Bread of Life if we are genuinely to be sustained. We long to give the world this Bread. As we take the Bread of Life to other persons, if they are physically hungry, we cannot ignore that need. We will meet that need and tell them that our concern for them is expressed in the name of the One who is the Bread of Life.

When we eat our daily meal, may it remind us of the One who gives us our food through his creative love. May this meal summon us to personal gratitude and concern for those who are hungry in our world. May our prayer of thanks for our daily bread also bring to our memory the Bread of Life. As we commune at the Table of our Lord and eat the bread that reminds us of the Bread, may we never forget that he also provides us our daily bread. My prayer is that our dinner table and the Table of the Lord will direct us to remember our Father who gives us every good gift out of his love for us. For this bread may we be eternally grateful.

NOTES

1 David H. C. Read, *Holy Common Sense* (Nashville: Abingdon Press, 1968), 50-51.

2 Maltbie D. Babcock, *Thoughts for Every-Day Living* (New York: Charles Scribner's Sons, 1901), 167.

3 George F. Vicedom, *A Prayer for the World* (Saint Louis: Concordia Publishing House, 1967), 93.

4 William Barclay, *The Gospel of Matthew* (Philadelphia: The Westminster Press, 1958), 1:217.

5 Joachim Jeremias, *The Prayers of Jesus* (London: SCM Press, 1976), 100.

6 Eduard Schweizer, *The Good News According to Matthew* (Atlanta: John Knox Press, 1977), 153.

7 Margaret Lee Runbeck, *Hope of Earth* (Boston: Houghton Mifflin Co., 1947).

8 William Osler, *A Way of Life* (Baltimore: The Remington-Putnam Book Co., 1932), 17-19.

9 Jeremias, 100-101.

THE NEED FOR FORGIVENESS

Matthew 6:12

Several years ago I had the good fortune of visiting the Coventry Cathedral in England. It was an interesting experience. When I entered the church, I discovered that it was contemporary in its architecture. During World War II, the original cathedral was bombed by the Nazis. The church and much of the town was destroyed in these bombings. There was no time to evacuate anybody from the city, and many lives were lost. When the new church was reconstructed, it was built around a part of the destroyed church. I entered a small courtyard where part of the old walls and a tower stood just as they were after being bombed in the war. Here one was reminded vividly of the cost of the war. Over to one side in the courtyard was a cross made from some of the timbers taken from the bombed-out building. On the cross were these words: "Father, forgive." Persons, who had known devastation firsthand, chose this symbolic way to express their forgiveness for those who had brought destruction on them during an awful time of war.

In the Lord's Prayer, the petition for forgiving follows immediately the one on giving. Forgiving and giving are rooted in our basic wants. We pray to God to give us bread to meet our physical needs. But life teaches us early the need to pray for forgiveness to meet our spiritual need. Our physical need drives us to bread. Our spiritual need drives us to ask for forgiveness. The physical and spiritual needs are intertwined. We ask for bread so we can be physically strong, but we also plead for forgiveness so that we might be spiritually strong. After the requirement of our body comes the need of our soul. But I wonder how many people pray with the same intensity for the forgiveness of their sins as they do for the meeting of their physical needs.

VARIED TRANSLATIONS OF THIS TEXT

Move with me now to look at this brief petition. We have to acknowledge the confusion in the Christian church about which text should be prayed here. In some traditions this petition reads, "Forgive us our *debts*." In other communities, Christians pray together, "Forgive us our *trespasses*." What are we to make of this? The Gospel of Matthew uses a Greek word that literally means "something which is owed." Its root meaning refers to an obligation, a debt, a duty, such as a moral, religious, or financial duty or debt a person has to fulfill. In Luke's gospel, the writer uses a familiar Greek word for sin that means, "missing the mark." When Tyndale translated Matthew's word, he was the first one to use the word "trespasses." "Trespasses," however, is another word altogether in Greek. It means to make a blunder, take a false step, or to make a slip, like a slip in grammar. The mistranslation of trespasses was carried forward by the King James Version and the Book of Common Prayer.

Some other Protestant traditions have continued to use this word to the present day. To be honest, it is a poor translation that has no support in the biblical text. But in some ways that entire debate is irrelevant, isn't it? Both Matthew and Luke, and even the incorrect translation, make the same basic thrust—you and I have committed some kind of wrong against God. The New English Bible reads, "Forgive us the wrongs we have done as we have forgiven those who have wronged us."

SINNERS WHO NEED FORGIVENESS

Let's make an examination of the petition itself. We have to begin with an acknowledgment that we are sinners in need of forgiveness. But not everyone is willing to begin there, are they? Sin is a meaningless word to some people.

LIFE IS FUTILE TO SOME

There are some who say, "What's this conversation about sin? What difference does it make? Life is utter nonsense anyway." They agree with the words from Ecclesiastes, "Vanity and vanity, all is vexation of the spirit" (Eccl 1:14). "What difference does life make anyway?" they ask. "We will all soon be dead."

Thomas Hardy's historical drama *The Dynasts* depicts the bloody era of the Napoleonic wars. The play itself is interesting, but one of the most intriguing features of the play is the commentary on the action by a chorus of spirits called the Pities and the Fates, who remain in the background. Looking down on Europe bathed in blood, the Pities ask the Fates: "What plan or purpose is being worked out through all this agony?" The reply of the Fates is:

No plan and no purpose, it is like the rest of human history, a tale told by a fool, full of sound and fury, signifying absolutely nothing. Round and round, in endless cycles of sorrow following sorrow, and sin that grows from sin, human history runs its course to nothingness at last. And all things in the end will be as though nothing had ever been.

These persons respond to life with an attitude of absolute futility. No matter what they do, they feel, it really makes no difference anyway. "It is all utter nonsense," they cry. Life is just a cul-de-sac, a dead-end street that leads nowhere.

SOME DENY THEY ARE SINNERS

Others deny that they are sinners. They don't want you to speak about that morbid topic, sin. "What do you mean by sinfulness?" they ask. "I am not a murderer. I have never robbed anybody. I have not committed adultery. I haven't done any of those awful things, therefore I am all right." Unfortunately, there is a host of people who deny any consciousness of sin. They may admit that they lie a bit, even cheat some on their taxes, even shoplift occasionally, or engage in some extramarital sex.

They feel that anything is right if you can get by with it. Something is dishonest only if you get caught at it. But these people still do not think of themselves as sinners. "That is a label for somebody else, not me," they cry. "What I do is really not that bad." They are unwilling to acknowledge that they are sinners, and almost seem to gloat in what they get away with. Television shows are rampant with this philosophy of life. Young people and too many adults buy into this philosophy and make it their daily companion.

Lucy is talking to Charlie Brown one day. "Do you know what the whole trouble with you is?" she asks. "The whole trouble with you is that you won't listen to the whole trouble with you!" Well, that is our problem too, isn't it? We don't want somebody telling us that we have weaknesses, and especially that we are sinners.

OTHERS ARE OBSESSED WITH GUILT

But there is the flip side to this view. Some people are deeply aware that they are sinners. They are so conscious of their failures and so obsessed with their guilt that they can hardly function as persons. They have committed some act, some wrong in their lives in the past that they feel has trapped them forever. They seem unable to find forgiveness. They feel like they are bound with a huge chain of garbage from their past, and they cannot get free. In his days as a young monk, Martin Luther was obsessed with his sense of sin and could not seem to experience forgiveness no matter how often he confessed his sins. Luther and persons like him long for a liberating word.

ACKNOWLEDGE YOUR SINFULNESS

The Scriptures and the reality of life both affirm that all have sinned and come short of the glory of God. To experience forgiveness, you and I have to begin with an honest confession that we have sinned. Do you honestly think you have never sinned? Do you mean that you have never said anything in your life that has hurt another person? Have you never at any moment in your life done some act that caused problems or difficulties for another person? Can you really say that you have never at any moment in your life thought or done anything that was offensive or wrong in any degree? Think about it! Be honest! We have all sinned. That is the point of beginning, if you are to know forgiveness.

You and I, if we are to find forgiveness, begin in the acknowledgment that we have sinned. No one can experience forgiveness if he or she is unwilling to acknowledge his or her sinfulness. Paul Tillich has written:

> There is no condition for forgiveness. But forgiveness could not come to us if we were not asking for it and receiving it. Forgiveness is an answer, the divine answer, to the question implied in our existence. An answer is an answer only for him who has asked, is aware of the question.[1]

You cannot find an answer to the question of sin if you are not aware of your need for an answer to that question. To pray, "forgive us the wrong we have done," is to acknowledge our sinfulness.

Deep down within us we know our guilt, and the burden of our sin hangs heavily upon us. The grand miracle of the Christian faith is that you and I can be forgiven. The power of sin and the burden of guilt can be removed through the marvelous grace of God. God is not only a giver but also a forgiver. This is the good news of our faith. "God shows his love for us in that while we were yet sinners Christ died for us" (Rom 5:8).

THE COSTLY NATURE OF SIN

We are also aware of the costly nature of sin and of forgiveness. You and I do not receive cheap grace from God. When we seek forgiveness, let it be with the acknowledgment of the dreadful nature of sinfulness. Once you and I commit an act of sin, it is a part of the stream of life. Sin has entered the current of life and we cannot retrieve it; we cannot take it back. We cannot undo the past. We cannot wash ourselves clean of sin by our own efforts. We cannot purge our souls of the damage we have done.

Francis of Assisi was approached one day by a woman in the village who told him of malicious gossip that she had spread about some of her neighbors in the community. She felt bad about it and wanted to know what she could do about it. He asked her to take some feathers and go into the village and place a feather on the doorstep of each person whom she had offended. She thought that was a rather strange request, but since this was a holy man, she agreed to follow his

suggestion. After she completed this task, she came back and indicated that she had followed his instructions. "Now go," he said, "and
gather the feathers and bring them to me." But when she went into
the village to try to find the feathers, she could not. The wind had
blown them away. "Neither can you take back those harmful words.
They are as irretrievable as feathers in the wind."

You and I cannot undo the wrong that we have done through our
sinning. This knowledge pushes us to the need for the Other—God,
who can bring us forgiveness and the opportunity to begin anew. This
is the Christian message of the grace of God. You and I cannot extri-
cate our debts. We cannot go back and undo all of our own wrongs
and set everything right. We come to God and ask forgiveness. "For
by grace are you saved" (Eph 2:5). "For God so loved the world that
he gave his only begotten son" (John 3:16).

Sin separates us from God, but Jesus bridged that chasm through
the cross to restore our broken relationship with God. In the central
stained glass window in the sanctuary of St. Matthews Baptist Church
in Louisville, Kentucky, is the cross of Christ with a lamb as the major
focus. This symbolizes "The Lamb which was slain from the foundation of the world" (Rev 13:8). Many churches have the cross at the
center of worship. This symbol is always before the congregation to
remind them of the grace of God and the costly nature of that love.
We cannot dismiss our sins and forgive ourselves. We cannot undo our
sins, but God can forgive us. And we can begin again.

WE CONTINUOUSLY PRAY FOR FORGIVENESS

The psalmist cried: "Create within me a clean heart, O God. " He
knew that he could not cleanse himself. He was dependent upon God.
But in thanksgiving for God's grace, he exclaimed: "Bless the Lord, O
my soul; and all that is within me, bless his holy name!… and forget
not all his benefits, who forgives all your iniquity" (Ps 103:1-2). All
that is within him—his heart, kidneys, mind, stomach ,and all the rest
of his body—join the Psalmist as he praises God for divine grace.

When we enter the presence of God and experience divine grace,
"the impossible happens," Gerhard Ebeling declares. "The man who
must need fall silent before God does so by opening his mouth to

God."[2] God is the one who cleanses us. God is the one who gives us, forgives us, heals us, and redeems us. God brings us forgiveness and freedom from our guilt and sin. "As far as the east is from the west, so far does he remove our transgressions from us" (Ps 103:12)

We not only need to pray daily for our bread, but we need to pray daily for forgiveness. We have not sinned just once in our lives. We continue to be sinners even as Christians. It is important for us to return again and again to the altar of God to ask God to forgive us our sins that we might continuously experience God's love and cleansing grace. We can thankfully acknowledge the reality of the forgiving grace of God.

WE RECEIVE FORGIVENESS BY FORGIVING OTHERS

"Forgive us our debts, wrongs, sins, trespasses—as we forgive others." In this petition, Jesus has taught us to pray not only for our own forgiveness, but indicates that our forgiveness is linked with our willingness to forgive others who have wronged us. Now, I don't know what you think about that. But it is rather disturbing to me. It is frightening to think that my forgiveness by God is somehow dependent on whether or not I can forgive other people. If that doesn't disturb you a bit, it should. Think for a moment. Have you ever harbored feelings of anger toward a person or held a grudge because of something somebody did to you? An unforgiving spirit cuts us off from the presence of God. Most of us would have to confess that we have had such feelings at one time or another. Unfortunately, this unforgiving attitude blocks our relationship with God.

The novelist, Robert Louis Stevenson, who was a very devout man, spent the last few years of his life on a small island where he went for health reasons. The family concluded each day with a time of devotion and ended with the Lord's Prayer. One night, after they had finished singing and the family was preparing to pray together the Lord's Prayer, Stevenson got up and left the room. His wife, knowing that her husband was not well, followed him out to see if he were sick. He told her that he was not ill, but that he had had feelings of hostility toward someone who had committed an unexpected treachery toward him. He readily acknowledged, "I am not yet fit to say, 'Forgive us our trespasses as we forgive those who trespass against us.'"

OUR ATTITUDE MAY BLOCK GOD'S CARE

There are times in your life and mine when our attitude toward other persons causes us spiritual problems. This petition is not some kind of transaction between God and humanity. Jesus is not saying, "If you do this for somebody else then God will do that for you." Jesus is not offering us some kind of bargain religion with a doctrine of works or merit. But it is a spiritual reality of life that, if you and I are unforgiving, we block God's ability to minister to us. Frank Stagg, the New Testament scholar, has expressed it this way: "It is not that God is unwilling to forgive the unforgiving but the condition of the unforgiving is such that they are incapable of receiving forgiveness. When a door is closed, it is closed from both sides."[3] When you and I have closed the door toward others, we also close it toward God.

One of the conditions of the spiritual life is that our attitude toward other people affects our attitude toward God. When you and I harbor feelings of revenge, or cling to hatreds and hostilities, or nurse old grudges, we block the avenue of our own forgiveness. If we assert, "I'll never forgive; I won't forget that," then we make it difficult to receive God's grace. Jesus clearly connected receiving with giving. "Inasmuch as you have done it unto the least of these, you have done it unto me" (Matt 25:45). "Blessed are the merciful, for they shall receive mercy" (Matt 5:7). "With what judgment you judge, you shall be judged" (Matt 7:2). Remember Jesus' words in another place: "If you forgive men their trespasses, your heavenly Father will also forgive you: But if you forgive not men their trespasses, neither will your Father forgive your trespasses" (Matt 6:14-15). It is a spiritual principle that the way we act toward others radically affects us. An unforgiving spirit closes the door against God, who is always seeking to forgive us. Forgiveness can enter a life only when that life is open. It is an inescapable principle that where forgiveness is concerned, there cannot be receiving without giving.

By the time Leonardo da Vinci, the famous artist, was in the process of painting the canvas of "The Last Supper," he had made many enemies and critics. When he painted the face of Judas, he placed on him the face of one of his most avowed critics. But when he tried to paint the face of Jesus, he found that he could not. That image continued to elude him. Finally he realized that his attitude of revenge toward his critic blocked his mind to Christ. So he painted through the antagonist face that he had put on Judas. After he put aside his feelings of revenge, he found that he was able to paint the face of Jesus easily.

When you and I harbor feelings of hatred, resentment, hostility, anger, and revenge toward others, God's grace cannot filter into our own lives. The parable of the unmerciful servant reminds us of the necessity of forgiving to receive forgiveness. We cannot forget the warning that Jesus directed toward us when he concluded the parable about a man who was unwilling to forgive his servant a small amount and therefore forfeited his right to be forgiven a large sum. "So likewise shall my heavenly Father do also unto you, if from your heart you forgive not every one his brother their trespasses" (Matt 18:35). When Peter asked Jesus, "Lord, how often shall my brother sin against me, and I forgive him? As many as seven times?" Jesus replied, "I do not say to you seven times, but seventy times seven" (Matt 18:21-22). Forgiveness does not keep count; it is without limits.

If we could know what goes on in somebody else's life, I wonder how much more understanding we might be of them. It is easy to be judgmental and assume that we know why another person has done what they did and be unforgiving. But if we only knew the burdens that individual bears, the hardships that weigh on them, the family crises, their stresses at work, their sense of inadequacy and insecurity, their health problems, etc., we would see them differently. If we could only walk in that person's shoes for a while, maybe we could be more understanding. Jesus instructs us to be more understanding of others, which will lead us to be more forgiving of others. Our refusal blocks our ability to receive God's grace.

Shakespeare has reminded us of the profound quality of mercy or forgiveness:

The quality of mercy is not strain'd;
It droppeth as the gentle rain from heaven
Upon the place beneath: it is twice blest:
It blesseth him that gives and him that takes:
'Tis mightiest in the mightiest; it becomes
The throned monarch better than his crown:
His sceptre shows the force of temporal power,
The attribute to awe and majesty,
Wherein doth sit the dread and fear of kings;
But mercy is above this sceptred sway,
It is enthroned in the hearts of kings,
It is an attribute to God himself;
And earthly power doth then show likest God's
When mercy seasons justice.

From *The Merchant of Venice*, Act IV, Scene 1, ll.184-197.

WE CAN BE FORGIVEN

The good news today is that we can be forgiven. You and I can personally experience the grace of God. If you have not known that grace, then this is the day you can receive the good news of God's forgiveness and start again. A man was once asked, "If you could have anything you wanted in life, what would you want it to be?" He answered, "To begin again." That is the good news of the gospel. You can begin again as a forgiven person. "As far as the east is from the west," God has removed your sins. Begin with compassion for yourself. Accept God's acceptance of you and then, in turn, forgive others. First forgive yourself. Now give that compassion away by forgiving others.

You and I join with hundreds of others as we lift up our hands and ask for forgiveness. This prayer links us with all humanity. All have sinned. Confess your sins and experience the grace of God. Having experienced God's grace, then harbor no secret chambers of hatred toward others but throw open the doors of your life so God's spirit can fill your life. We find grace in being forgiven and in forgiving others. Be graceful toward others, as you have experienced God's grace. May you know the grace of your own sins, which have been forgiven, and the grace of forgiving others. May we all learn to pray meaningfully, "Forgive us the wrongs we have done as we have forgiven those who wronged us."

NOTES

[1] Paul Tillich, *The New Being* (New York: Charles Scribner's Sons, 1955), 9.

[2] Gerhard Ebeling, *On Prayer* (Philadelphia: Fortress Press, 1966), 99.

[3] Frank Stagg, "Matthew," *The Broadman Bible Commentary*, vol. 18 (Nashville: Broadman Press, 1969), 116.

FORTIFIED BY GOD

Matthew 6:13

The man looked up at me and commented, "Pastor, I just do not understand this petition in the Lord's Prayer. Why should we have to ask God not to lead us into temptation? Is God somehow going to trick or seduce us into sinning?" This man's observation is a good one, isn't it? As we examine this petition, we have to acknowledge that it is strange, puzzling, and rather perplexing. Does God tempt us? Will God lead us into temptation that God has asked us to avoid?

The Lord's Prayer has three petitions that focus on our needs. The first one is concerned with the present— "Give us our daily bread." Then our prayer looks back to the past— "Forgive us our sins." This petition looks toward the future— "Bring us not into temptation." We all have concerns about the future to some degree, don't we? As we look to the future, we wonder about our personal health and that of our family. We have questions about job security, financial security, and about the happiness of our family.

THE SERIOUS NATURE OF EVIL

I wonder how many people are seriously troubled about the temptations that they may have to face tomorrow. I think most people would say: "Well, I think I can handle whatever will come." Most of us really do not believe that our temptations will be so frightening or perplexing that we cannot deal with them. We take temptations too lightly and assert unrealistically our own strength.

But that is not the New Testament picture. The New Testament depicts a raging battle between good and evil. Men and women are engaged in a constant struggle with unseen forces of evil. The New Testament takes this evil force so seriously that it warns the Christian that this enemy has the power to destroy our soul. In this petition Jesus warns his disciples that they need to pray that they will not be led into temptations that may destroy them.

GOD, DON'T SEDUCE US!

Let's face the question at the beginning by looking at this troublesome phrase and asking in a straightforward way: "Does this petition teach us that God may seduce or trick us, therefore, we have to pray, 'God, don't entrap us?'" Is George Buttrick correct in asking, "Must we beseech him not to act like a devil?"[1] Yet, that is what this petition sounds like, isn't it? We are astonished and troubled by it.

INSIGHT FROM THE JEWISH PERSPECTIVE

Let me suggest that we back up for a moment. Maybe we can get some insight into this petition if we have a better understanding of the Jewish perspective on life. To the Jewish mind, everything that happened had its source in God. It didn't make any difference what happened; ultimately it came from God. When you read the Old Testament, you will come across accounts about a person deciding to take some course of action. He always attributes his decision to God. The Old Testament story does not depict an individual saying, "I have decided I will go on a journey to another country. I have carefully looked at the situation and believe that is the thing I should do." No, rather than that, it usually reads: "God led Abraham, Jacob, etc. to go to a new land." Or, "The Lord said to Abraham, Moses, or Jacob, 'Get up with your family and go to a certain place.'" At other times, the Old Testament uses expressions like; "The word of the Lord came unto...." The New Testament record of Jesus' time in the wilderness does not read that Jesus decided to go into the wilderness for a few days, but that "the Spirit 'led' him into the wilderness." To the Jewish mind, no decision or action was made or taken apart from the guidance of God. God's leadership was dominant in all matters.

From the Jewish perspective, this was true even in the people's understanding of evil. They believed that God was the creator of all of life. Although God had not created evil per se, God had created a world where the possibility of evil existed. God created men and women with free will, and with that freedom goes the possibility of choosing evil. Look, for example, at the Old Testament story about Pharaoh and the children of Israel. The writer does not say that Pharaoh decided to kill the children of Israel, but that "God hardened his heart." "Wait a minute!" we want to say. "What does that mean?" Does that imply that Pharaoh was not responsible for his own actions? Does this statement mean that God made him choose evil? Oh, no, not to the Jew! What the writer was really saying was this: Pharaoh was given free will by God to choose good or evil. Pharaoh was responsible for his own decision. But as Creator, God was ultimately responsible, because God gave Pharaoh his free will. This did not mean that God made him choose evil, but that God created a world where such a choice was a real possibility. In Jewish thought, whatever happened ultimately originated from God.

NOTE VARIOUS TRANSLATIONS OF THIS PETITION

Turn with me now and see if we can get any help from the various translations of this petition. Scholars have tried to address the obvious problem in this petition by giving various renderings as they have translated it. In the Synodal Version, widely used in French-speaking countries, this text has been translated: "Abandon us not to temptation." A variant reading states, "Put us not to the test." The J. B. Phillips translation reads, "Keep us clear of temptation, and save us from evil."

William Barclay has rendered this text, "Do not submit us to any time of testing, but rescue us from the Evil One." The translation by Charles Williams resembles the one by Barclay: "And do not let us be subjected to temptation, but save us from the evil one." The Richard Weymouth version reads, "And bring us not into temptation, but rescue us from the Evil One." *Good News for Modern Man* reads, "Do not bring us to hard testing, but keep us safe from the Evil One." *The Geneva Bible* states, "Expose us not to temptation." Augustine, many years ago, translated this text, "Do not allow us to be led into temptation." A. T. Robertson, the Baptist New Testament scholar, rendered it, "And bring us not into temptation." The *New English Bible* reads, "And do not bring us to the test, but save us from the evil one."

As you can see, there are a variety of ways you can render this particular verse. The root idea for temptation is "test, try, or trial." No translation of this verse changes the involvement of God. In all of these renderings, whether they read "lead," "bring," "abandon," "submit," etc., God is still recognized as the source behind everything that happens.

TESTING GIVES US CHOICES

Through God's permissive will, God gives all persons the opportunity to make choices. God does not directly tempt us, but God does permit temptation or testing. A clear fact of life is that we are being tested at every moment. The reality of life is that there could be no possibility of good without the possibility of evil. This is the kind of universe God has created. You cannot tell whether you are really honest if there is never any test of dishonesty. Can there be any real test of courage without the possibility of being a coward? We know the meaning of good health because we recognize the danger of illness.

WE CONSTANTLY FACE TESTING

Life is made up of testing. You and I as parents cannot shield our children from all of the hard knocks of life. It is a mistake to try. Life is filled with all kinds of tests. Children are tested as they try to learn how to crawl or walk. We constantly face testing in school, as we attempt to relate to other people, or learn a skill or train for a vocation, or do our daily work. We are continuously tested by one thing, person, event, circumstance, or another. God has not sheltered us from the possibility of testing. Just as a child has to be exposed to the test of life to grow, God permits temptations—testing—to come our way so we might grow.

James has given us an interesting insight into this verse in his small epistle when he wrote: "Let no one say when he is tempted, 'I am tempted of God,' for God cannot be tempted with evil and he himself tempts no one" (Jas 1:13). James' observation is helpful here. God does not tempt us, but God has created the possibility of evil or good in the world. You and I have to make choices. We have to learn to live in a world where we are exposed to evil choices. This does not mean that God deliberately makes us choose evil or that God tempts us to do something wrong. But God has created a world where the possibility of our being tempted is a reality.

The drama of the book of Job illustrates this in a magnificent way. The man Job has everything he could desire in life. Satan appears on the scene and asserts to God, "Job only loves you because he is healthy, wealthy, and wise. Let me test his mettle and I will show you that he doesn't have the stuff that will make him endure." In this dramatic book, God gives Satan the freedom to test Job.

Job's tests are a reality of life. Temptations or tests do come into our lives. God has created a world where the freedom of this testing is simply a fact. Just as gold is refined in fire, so our lives are refined in the fiery times of testing. God is primarily interested in developing our character, our authentic self, and not merely in making life comfortable or rosy. The universe provides the testing to make us into the kind of persons God created us to be in the first place.

A Permissive Imperative

Tests of all kinds do come. This petition is what A. T. Robertson has called "a permissive imperative."[2] God permits the possibility of temptation and evil to test the fiber of our being. Growth cannot come without some testing. Nevertheless, we may pray: "Do not put me to the test." But testing will come.

On May 25, 1979, a DC-10 jumbo jet crashed near Chicago, killing the 274 people aboard. Until September 11, 2001, it was the worst plane crash in the U. S. history. The engine on the left wing fell off the plane just as it was taking off at O'Hare International Airport. Several weeks later all DC-10 jets were grounded by the FAA because fractures in bushings and bolts, cracks, and signs of metal fatigue in bulkheads were found during inspections. It is uncertain at this time exactly what caused these failures. But one thing is certain. Airplanes were not made to be admired on the ground; they were designed to fly. If the plane cannot stand the stress and pressure of flight, it is of no real value. It was made to fly.

Tempting stresses will come into every life. Whether you have the stuff within to enable you to stand in the time of testing will be the determining factor. As you are sifted or tested by the storms and trials of life, your ability to stand will be determined by the way you are made "within." You were not created to be removed from the "tests" of life but to live creatively within them. If you are rooted and grounded in God, life's tests will not bring you down. Instead, you will grow stronger through them and achieve deeper wisdom and maturity.

A PRAYER FOR FAITHFULNESS

Look further at this petition and observe that it is a prayer for faithfulness. We all face temptations and suffering. This prayer is a cry that we will not be thrown into circumstances where we will not be able to maintain control. Who among us at some time or another has not felt thrust into a time of testing so strong that he or she was going to be swept away by the raging stream of temptation around them? Caught in its powerful current, we are frightened, even terrified of it. The warning from Paul needs to ring in our ears: "Let any one who thinks that he stands take heed lest he fall" (1 Cor 10:12).

ARE WE LED INTO, UNTO, OR TO?

Some scholars have suggested that help in understanding this petition might be found in the distinction between the words *into* and *unto* or *to*. A person can be led *into* something or up *to* it. There is a real difference in a person entering *into* the kingdom of God or being brought *unto* it. When we enter the kingdom of God, we are a part of it and give our allegiance to its claims. But to come *unto* it is still not to be a real part of it or its demands. We cannot really pray that we not be led *unto* temptation, but we can realistically pray that we might not enter *into* temptation and come under its power and control. We may be led *unto* the edge of the far country, but we do not have to take the journey *into* that wilderness. God will expose us *unto* testing, but we do not have to yield by giving *into* it.

Jon Lochman believes that the correct interpretation of this petition is "Let us not be caught in the sphere of temptation" or "Do not let us correspond or confound to temptation." He sees this interpretation confirmed in the fact that the New Testament offers us a positive alternative to the sixth petition, which is entering the kingdom of God (Matt 19:23).[3]

WE CANNOT AVOID ALL TEMPTATIONS

Temptations of all kinds do come, don't they? We cannot avoid them completely. Temptations may come to us at the point of our selfishness, pride, or appetites. Temptations may arise to test our bodies, minds, spirits, or our relationships to other persons. Temptations sometimes come at our weakest points, and/or other occasions at our strongest points. Temptations are such deceivers. They say to us, "Oh, now friend, don't worry about this one." "Everybody does it." "I'm only human." "This really won't harm you." "After all, be a man or woman. Prove yourself. Show them that you are somebody."

SIN DISGUISES ITSELF

Sin disguises itself in deceitful masks and lures us into its grasp as it continuously lurks in the shadows of our lives. A friend or an enemy, a new opportunity or old habit may open the door to temptation. You may walk down the same pathway again and again and feel that you are really in control of the situation, and suddenly its ugly hand grabs you and pulls you down into the pits of destruction. You may think that you can stop doing whatever you are doing anytime you want. So, you continue to drink too much, keep on using drugs, continue to pilfer a small amount of money from your firm, or persist in cheating on your wife or husband. What you do, you say to yourself, really doesn't harm anyone and it's just a little here and there. You go on flirting at the edge of temptation, thinking that you have the power to draw back and stop any time you want. But do you?

In one of Charles Schultz's comic strips, Lucy is talking to Linus. "Linus, there's still time for you to make a New Year's resolution to give up that blanket." "You know," Linus says. "You're right! I think if

I'm ever going to get rid of it NOW is the time!" As he throws his blanket away, he says: "So I'll just throw it away and be done with it once and for all." He stands there with his hands empty. But when you look at the blanket lying on the floor, you can't help noticing that a string is attached to it. One scene passes after another without a word being spoken. Perspiration begins to break out on his head. Finally he pulls on the string until the blanket is back in his arms. He hugs it to himself and observes, "Never believe anything I say."[4]

What a powerful symbol for the deception of sin. "I can stop any-time I want," we say. "I can let go." "I can cut it off." Yet we attach strings to our temptations that pull us back into the old ways. We cannot really stop. Our old attachments draw us back again and again to the way that leads to destruction. Everyone has an Achilles' heel. No one is immune to temptation.

PRAY THAT WE NOT COMMIT APOSTASY

Some scholars are convinced that the major thrust of this passage is not concerned with minor sins. They believe that its primary focus is on faithfulness. Our prayer is that you and I not commit apostasy. Joachim Jeremias, Professor of New Testament at the University of Gottingen, Germany, has stated it forcefully in these words: "O Lord, preserve us from falling away, from apostasy." In a slightly different form, he states the same truth. "Dear Father, this one request grant us: preserve us from falling away from Thee."[6] If this is the case, our prayer here is: "Oh, Lord don't bring me to that kind of test where I might fall away from the faith." This is the ultimate test. All other temptations are only a part of a deeper test—our relationship to God.

Jesus experienced this kind of temptation when he was tested for forty days in the wilderness. The temptation to turn stones into bread, to throw himself down from the temple (the appeal of magic), and to accept the offer to control all of the kingdoms of the world were tests to persuade Jesus to be faithless. All three tests challenged Jesus to use his religious powers for selfish ends. If Jesus had yielded to these temp-tations, he would have turned away from God and worshiped at the shrine of Satan. Jesus overcame—withstood—his temptations, because he remained close to God. Jesus warned his disciples again and again to be faithful unto death. He knew firsthand the seriousness of the challenge to fall away from what one believed.

There is a scene in the novel *Barabbas* by Par Lagerkvist that depicts the testing of two men's faith. Barabbas, you remember, was the man who was set free by the crowd as Pilate offered them a choice, and our Lord was condemned to the cross to die. Barabbas was later arrested again. This time he was made a Roman slave and sent to Cyprus and forced to work in the copper mines. While working in the mines, he met an Armenian slave named Sahak who was a deeply committed Christian.

Each one of the slaves wore a disk around his neck that indicated that he belonged to Caesar. On the back of his disk, Sahak had scratched "Christos Jesus" to indicate that Christ was his Lord. Saying that he too wanted to follow the Galilean, Barabbas asked that his disk be inscribed with the name of Jesus. Unfortunately, their conversation was overheard and they were turned in to the supervisor, who took them to the governor.

The governor warned them that Caesar was god and they could not have any gods before Caesar. To deny that Caesar was god, he told them, was punishable by death. When Sahak was asked about the inscription on the back of his disk, he replied that it was his God. He was told that he could escape punishment by death if he would deny Christ.

Then the governor turned to Barabbas and asked him if Christ was his God. Barabbas shook his head. "He isn't?" asked the governor. "Why do you wear his name on your disk then?" Barabbas remained silent. "Is he your God?" he asked. "Isn't that what this inscription means?" Then Barabbas spoke so softly that his words were almost not audible. "I have no god," Barabbas answered. Turning to Sahak again, the governor told him, "If you renounce your faith no harm shall come to you. Will you do it?" "I cannot," Sahak replied. The governor then gave the order that Sahak be taken out and crucified. As Sahak was being led away, the governor observed: "Extraordinary man."

The governor then took a knife and, holding Barabbas' disk in one hand, he scratched through the name of Jesus. "There's really no need," he observed, "as you don't believe in him in any case." He commended Barabbas for being a sensible man and ordered that he be given a better job in the mines.[6]

A lot of people have scratched through the name of Jesus Christ, which at one time they pronounced with their lips. Many have fallen away from him. Across our country they have fallen away in droves. All you have to do is examine church rolls and note hundreds, and in some congregations thousands of people, who put their names at one time on that church roll but never darken the doors of the church today. They allow vacations, football games, recreation, weekend trips, visitation, and television to dominate their lives. These persons may not have deliberately turned away from Christ, but the other matters of life simply crowded him out. The other matters of importance became their new god. Sometimes, even without realizing it, they have committed apostasy. They have not fallen away from God by some big temptations. But they have gradually, ever so casually, given in to the test of their character. Through busyness, apathy, and preoccupation, they have slipped away.

THE DEMAND OF THE GOSPEL

The hard sayings of Jesus call us to consider the uncompromising demands of the gospel. "What shall it profit a man if he gains the whole world and loses his own soul?" (Mark 8:36). "Do not fear those who kill the body but cannot kill the soul, rather fear him who can deliver both soul and body in hell" (Matt 10:28). Jesus said, "If your right hand offends you, cut it off" (Matt 5:30). "If your right eye offends you, pluck it out" (Matt 5:29). "He that loves father and mother more than me is not worthy of me" (Matt 10:37). What message is Jesus trying to tell us in these offensive sayings? The Christian way will be hard and strenuous. He does not pretend that his way will be soft and easy. He exposes his disciples to the sandpaper edge of the gospel. To endure, a disciple will have to be faithful.

In the Garden of Gethsemane Jesus prayed agonizingly to know God's will as he faced the cross. When he first arrived at the garden, he told his disciples, "Watch and pray that you may not enter into temptation" (Luke 22:40). After he finished praying, he warned them again, "Rise and pray that you may not enter into temptation" (Luke 22:46). What temptation? The temptation to turn away from him in the time of testing.

Simply having one's name on a church roll, or having walked down a church aisle someplace in the past does not make a person genuinely committed to Jesus Christ. Real faith will be seen in a changed life and in the way that person lives each day. One of the worst lies of the church is for a person to assume that because his or her name is on a church roll somewhere or they *may* have made some kind of statement at one time in the past, then they are surely Christian. But, if their life gives no evidence of Christ-like characteristics, how can they make such a claim? "He that endureth to the end," Jesus said, "will be saved" (Matt 10:22*).* "You shall know my disciples by their fruits" (Matt 7:16).

GOD, DELIVER US FROM EVIL

This petition concludes, "Deliver us from evil," or "Deliver us from the evil one." Here is a clear acknowledgment that you and I do not have the power within to deliver ourselves. The strength to overcome evil is beyond our own resources. "Deliver us," we pray. Only God can deliver us. We are not adequate to combat such power alone. We turn to God who alone is able to deliver us.

THE AWESOME POWER OF EVIL

Through this petition, Jesus also acknowledges the awesome power of evil. The New Testament rings with vivid words depicting the terrible power of evil. It uses such images as "Principalities and powers," "The Anti-Christ," "rulers of darkness," "messengers of Satan," the Destroyer," "Satan, the father of lies and deception," "the Evil One," "the Adversary," and "the "Destroyer." Paul often used the phrase "principalities and powers" to denote the cosmic dimension of the power of evil.

You don't think evil is real? Tell that to the relatives in Ohio and Kentucky after Donald Harvey confessed that he killed dozens of their loved ones in hospitals and nursing homes. You don't think evil is real?

Tell that to the parents of the young child who contracted AIDS through a blood transfusion several years ago. Tell the parents of the teenagers who were killed by fellow students in Littleton, Colorado, that evil is not real. Tell the families of those who are dead or fleeing for their lives in Kosovo that evil is not real. You don't think evil is real? Tell that to the parents whose young son committed suicide or to the young man who is in the hospital today because he was in the woods in Vietnam when our own planes dropped defoliating chemicals on them. You don't think evil is real? Tell that to the families of those onboard four terrorist-held flights on September 11. You don't think evil is real? Look around you and within your own heart.

Paul reminds us that we are not contending merely against flesh and blood. We might be able to handle that struggle. But we are engaged in a battle with "principalities and powers and the spiritual hosts of wickedness in heavenly places" (Eph 6:12). For strength for this warfare, we turn to God. Dietrich Bonhoefferhas stated this truth vividly in the following lines:

> The Bible is not like a book of edification, telling us many stories of men's temptations and their overcoming. To be precise, the Bible tells only two temptation stories, the temptation of the first man and the temptation of Christ, that is the temptation which led to man's fall, and the temptation which led to Satan's fall. All other temptations in human history have to do with those two stories of temptation. Either we are tempted in Adam or we are tempted in Christ. Either the Adam in me is tempted—in which case we fall. Or the Christ in us is tempted—in which case Satan is bound to fall.[7]

GOD PROVIDES RESOURCES

Fortunately, we do not have to rely upon our own resources in our times of testing. We can turn to the presence of God to deliver us. God has already made provisions for us. We draw our strength from God who can deliver us. We are not alone in our temptations, tests, or trials. With the psalmist we can affirm: "Yea, though I walk through the valley of the shadow of death, I will fear no evil; for thou art with

me" (Ps 23:4). With Paul we testify, "I can do all things through Christ who strengthens me" (Phil 4:13). In another powerful passage that he wrote to the Corinthians, Paul gives us helpful encouragement. "No temptation has overtaken you that is not common to man. God is faithful, and he will not let you be tempted beyond your strength, but with the temptation will also provide the way of escape, that you may be able to endure it" (1 Cor 10:13). For every moral trial or test, God provides an alternative. Every temptation provides an opportunity to choose good as well as evil. But the most assuring word is that you and I are not left alone in our temptation.
God stands with us.

Jesus Christ, our high priest, knows our struggle and is ready to assist us. He not only knows our conflict, but helps us bear the burden of our difficult load. The writer of the book of Hebrews expressed this truth in these words of assurance: "For ours is not a high priest unable to sympathize with our weaknesses, but one who, because of his likeness to us, has been tested every way, only without sin. Let us therefore boldly approach the throne of our gracious God, where we may receive mercy and in his grace find timely help" (Heb 4:15-16).

A minister visited a bedridden member in his congregation one day. At one time she had a bright sunny faith, but during her time of illness, her faith had gone under a dark cloud. She looked up at him and said, "I don't think that I have any real faith left nowadays or any true love to Christ whatever." Her minister went over to the window and wrote some words on a piece of paper and then brought them over to the woman. She looked at the words he had written. "I do not love the Lord Jesus." "Now, my dear friend, you just sign that." "I can't sign that," she cried. "It's not true! I'd be torn in pieces before I'd sign that." "But you said it just now," he answered. "You know you said it." "Ah," she responded, "but I could not put my hand to it." "Well then," he observed, "I suspect you do love Him after all." "Yes, yes," she exclaimed. "I see it now! I do love Him—Christ knows I love Him!"

Sometimes in the pits of despair, crushed under the load of heavy burdens and difficulties, and when the testing seems so hard, we feel like we cannot make it, and we are not sure if we really love God. I believe you love him more than you realize. But be assured of this. God loves you, and it is God who will deliver you. A beautiful paraphrase of this sixth petition is found in the eleventh canto of Dante's *Purgatory*:

Our virtue which so soon doth harm receive,
Put not to peril with our ancient Foe;
But from his evil sting deliverance give.

Let us pray then, "Lord bring us not to the time of testing but deliver us from evil."

NOTES

[1] George A. Buttrick, *So We Believe, So We Pray* (New York: Abingdon Press, 1951), 206.

[2] Archibald T. Robertson, *Word Pictures in the New Testament* (Nashville: Broadman Press, 1930), 1:54.

[3] Jan Milic Lochman, *The Lord's Prayer* (Grand Rapids MI: William B. Eerdmans Publishing Co.), 145-146.

[4] Robert L. Short, *The Parables of Peanuts* (New York: Harper & Row, 1968), 86.

[5] Joachim Jeremias, *The Prayers of Jesus* (London: SCM Press, 1976), 106.

[6] Par Fabian Lagerkvist, *Barabbas* (New York: Random House, 1951), 141-147.

[7] Dietrich Bonhoeffer, *Temptation* (London: SCM Press, 1955), 14.

DOXOLOGY ON OUR LIPS

Matthew 6:13

In many translations of the Scripture, the latter part of verse thirteen, "Thine is the kingdom and the power and the glory forever," is put in a footnote. This verse is restricted to a footnote because it is not found in most ancient manuscripts. Most scholars consider these words not to be authentically from Jesus. The earliest record of these words was found in an ancient manuscript called the *Didache*, which is from the early part of the second century. These words are not a part of Luke's gospel. Luke ends the prayer with, "Deliver us from evil."

THE PEOPLE'S DOXOLOGY

If these are not the original words of Jesus, whose are they? Why, they are the response of the early church's congregation to the prayer of Christ. They were likely written in the margin of some ancient manuscript as a record of what the early church repeated each time this prayer was prayed in their churches. "Thine is the kingdom and the power and the glory forever, Amen" is the response of the people. It is their doxology.

The book of Chronicles relays David's praise for the response of the Jewish nation when they were asked to bring gifts for the building of the temple. The same doxology located in Chronicles is also recorded in the seventy-second Psalm. Here it is the ascription of praise and adoration by the congregation. "Blessed be the name and the glory of his kingdom forever" (1 Chron 16:36).

AN AUDACIOUS CLAIM

When the early church responded to the Lord's Prayer in this way, it was a statement of audacious faith. It is hard for us to imagine that they could shout, "For thine is the kingdom and the power and glory," in the face of the might of the Roman Empire. They heralded these words at the height of Greek culture and philosophy. They shouted them with their knowledge of the tradition and laws of ancient Judaism. Why? Because they believed that Jesus Christ was risen from the dead. Their belief in the resurrection of Christ totally transformed them. This group of peasants, fishermen, and slaves shouted these words with a cry of unrestrained assurance. The affirmation that Christ will reign was a doxology that voiced their total confidence in God.

This doxology resounded like the sound of a trumpet and the clash of cymbals proclaiming that Christ was risen. When early Christians met, one would often say to a fellow Christian, "Christ is risen." The other would respond, "Christ is risen indeed." The significance of this conclusion to the Lord's Prayer reminds us that the God to whom we pray is the source of all power and that the God to whom we pray requires not merely a repetition but a response. It is not enough just to recite the Lord's Prayer. Our Lord expects a response from us.

On the Mount of Olives in Jerusalem, there is a small church called Paternoster. This church is reputed to have been built on the site where Jesus taught his disciples the Lord's Prayer. The walls in this church bear copies of the Lord's Prayer in the languages of almost every known race in the world. Through the centuries this prayer has become the prayer of persons around the world. We have and continue to join voices with millions of others when we pray: "Our Father."

THINE IS THE KINGDOM

Look now at the meaning of this response. The doxology begins with "Thine is the kingdom." The world has known many different kinds of kingdoms. When this prayer was first voiced, the Holy Roman Empire ruled the world. Later the British Empire spread its rule across the land and seas. The Third Reich of Germany reigned briefly. Many other kingdoms have come and gone around the world. But this prayer affirms that the kingdom that will endure is God's kingdom. Although sin and evil are ever-present realities, it is God who reigns and rules in the hearts and minds of all persons and preserves us from temptation, assuring us that we will be delivered from the Evil One.

Our country has imprinted on its coins and paper money the words, "In God We Trust." That declaration is supposed to be an affirmation that the ultimate source of our allegiance is never first to America but to God. But can we genuinely declare that God's kingdom is the dominant force in our lives?

An ancient psalmist voiced praise for the King in these words:

Who is the king of glory?
The Lord, strong and mighty.
The Lord, mighty in battle.
The Lord of hosts, he is the king of glory. (Ps 24:8)

THE KINGDOM OF GOD IS WITHIN

Where is the kingdom of God? The kingdom of God is located wherever the King is. Jesus was once asked by the Pharisees when the kingdom of God would come. He responded by saying, "The kingdom of God is not coming with signs to be observed; nor will they say, 'Lo, here it is!' or 'There!' for behold the kingdom of God is in the midst of you" (Luke 17:20-21). Wherever Jesus Christ is, there is his kingdom. Why are some people unable to see the kingdom? Why? Because they are outside the kingdom. A person can only see the kingdom from within. The mystery of the kingdom of God is that only those within the kingdom can recognize it.

The stained glass windows in a church might serve as an example for us. A stained glass window was not meant to be viewed from the exterior. Their beauty can really be seen only from within as the sun shines through the various pieces of colored glass. If one stands on the outside of a church building, the stained glass will be obscured. The images on the glass can truly be seen only from within.

As followers of Jesus Christ, we are able to see his kingdom because of our perspective. Christ is in our lives, and we are in his kingdom. Having entered his kingdom, we are then able to "see" it. Where our Lord is present, his kingdom is a reality. His kingdom may be visible in this church, or in a church across the world. His kingdom may be in the hearts and lives of a people who cannot even have a church building where they are. But they pray together as a "church" to the Lord, and where he is present, his kingdom is there.

THE KINGDOM IS A PRESENT REALITY

But note, the church's doxology declares, "Thine *IS* the kingdom." Not that the kingdom will be or that it was, but the kingdom of God *is* a present reality. This petition speaks of what is and always has been. The kingdom of God has always existed. Jesus Christ came that we might understand the reign of God and enter into it. When the devil showed Jesus the kingdoms of this world and promised them to him if he would fall down and worship him, that was a lie. He did not possess the kingdoms of this world to give. "The earth is the Lord's."

GOD'S KINGDOM

Note also the phrase, "*Thine* is the kingdom." Remember it is God's kingdom. Many are unable to accept God's rule. Politicians, dictators, union leaders, industrial workers, laborers, entertainers, and many others claim that the earth is theirs. But the ancient Scriptures remind us that "the earth is the Lord's and the fullness thereof." Everything ultimately belongs to God. It is God's kingdom. It is God who rules. All that we have, we must acknowledge belongs to God.

I read about a man who was converted and joined a small church. He and his wife were illiterate, but they loved their church and their Lord. One night they came to church and noticed that all the men were wearing red jerseys with some words on them. Being unable to read, this couple did not know what they said. But the husband felt out of place because he did not have a red jersey. His wife went out and bought a red jersey for her husband. She decided to put some letters on it like she had seen the others wearing.

Not being able to read or write, she simply copied some letters from a sign which she saw across the street from where they lived. Neither of them knew that these men wore these jerseys because they were members of the church's softball team. Their names and number were inscribed on the back. The next Sunday night, when this convert came to church, he had on his new red jersey with letters across the back which read, "Under new management."

How appropriate for a new convert! When one was outside the kingdom of God and now has been brought into it, he or she is now under the management and direction of God. "For thine is the kingdom." To pray those words is to acknowledge who is in charge of our lives.

ULTIMATE POWER BELONGS TO GOD

Move a step further and notice that we pray, "For thine is the kingdom and the *power*." Too many people seem to hunger for power, don't they? We see the quest for power all around us. We speak of political, military, and monetary power. We also have heard about atomic power, black power, senior power, and the corruption of power—to be in charge of something—to say that they have got control. The hunger to dominate is an all-consuming drive for some.

Many years ago a group of slaves were chained to the bottom of a ship as they were being transported to a distant land where they would be put on an auction block. One day one of the guards got too close to one of the slaves who was a giant of a man. The giant struck him with one blow and killed him. He then took the keys from the murdered guard and unlocked the chains on his ankles. Following his own freedom, he set the other captives free. All of the slaves slipped quietly up to the deck of the ship where they overpowered the crew and killed all of them.

Now they had their freedom. "They were free," they thought. They could now go wherever they wanted. But none of them knew how to navigate a ship. They had noticed that the captain and the crew often gathered around a small instrument that was called a compass. The slaves thought that this instrument was their god. So they knelt down before the compass, worshipped it, and prayed that it would guide them home. When it did not, the rebels smashed it. They thought they were free but they were not. A few hours before they had been bound in chains, now they were hopelessly lost.

Throughout the world, people grasp for power. Some become tyrants. Others use their wealth or some kind of force to dominate others. But they only think they are in charge of their lives. They have forsaken the real source of life's power—God. Years ago Cannon Streeter gave a definition of power that I have always liked. "Power," he said, "is the ability to accomplish purpose." What is the end goal of your power? The proper use of power depends on how a person uses that power. When a person uses power in a corrupt way, that is destructive. What is the reason we can trust God's power? It is because God's power is consistent with God's purpose.

What is the goal of God's power? Is it to crush us, to destroy us? No, the purpose of his power is to love us, redeem us, and restore us to the reason we were created. One of the most striking examples of the use of power is given when Jesus washes the disciples' feet. "Knowing that all power was his," the Scripture says. "Knowing that *all* power was his, he took a towel and a basin." The eternal God of the universe came through Jesus Christ to let us know that his power is to serve, redeem, and make us whole. Through the cross—humanity's worst destruction of God's love—the eternal God revealed divine concern, grace, and power.

Ultimate power belongs only to God. All human life is fragile. The strongest person and the greatest empire come to an end. How could Paul and Silas, who were thrown into a jail because of their faith and threatened with death, sing praises to God at midnight? How? Because they knew that the power of Rome was not ultimate power. They knew that Rome might destroy their bodies, but it could not destroy their souls or spirits. Whatever harm Rome did to them could not ultimately destroy them.

GOD'S POWER CHANGES US

God's power is also transforming. The word "power" in Greek is the root for our English words that mean dynamic or dynamite. When God's power comes into a life, it never leaves that person the same again. God's power changes us. God's power works in our lives to remake us into the divine image so that we will live more like God.

Many years ago in Bolivia a small church was constructed in a mining community. The congregation used whatever material they could find. Much of the wood was taken from the odds and ends of crating boxes that had been used for shipping by several large firms. The unpainted pulpit was constructed from one packing crate. The first time the minister walked into the pulpit, he noticed the words stenciled on the old crate: "Explosivos Peligrosos"—"Dangerous Explosives."

Isn't the word of God always dangerous and explosive as it comes into a life to transform it? When God comes into our lives, we are never the same again. God explodes our old wineskins with the power of the divine presence. The ultimate power of God is at work to create us and recreate us in God's own image. We pray for this change when we utter: "For thine is the kingdom and the power."

THE GLORY OF GOD

Go another step and hear not only, "For thine is the kingdom and the power"—but also "and the glory." What is the glory of God? The glory of God as depicted in the Scriptures is both radiant and terrible. God's majesty is so mysterious that we can never fully comprehend it. To speak of God's glory is to be aware of God's majesty and the honor we owe God. Ezekiel was the first ancient writer to describe God as inexpressible light and brilliance. No one can really comprehend God's glory. Do you remember the record of Moses asking God, "Show me your glory"? But God told him, "You can't look upon me and live." God let the goodness of the divine presence pass before Moses, so he could see the "backsides" of God.

But isn't that the way most of us have sensed God? We never see anything but a reflection of God. We can't look upon God's glory and live. We may see God reflected through his creation in the grandeur of the mountains, the flow of the rivers, in the changing autumn leaves, in the new life that comes in the springtime, in the mystery and radiance of a sunset or sunrise. Through the reflective nature of God, we perceive something about God's glory. The glory of God is always beyond our description. Sometimes we praise God with our lips and sing our doxologies and adoration unto God. At other times, we can only kneel in silence before that glory.

THE PEOPLE RESPOND

The early church concluded their doxology by saying "Amen." The word "amen" was on the lips of Jesus quite a few times in the gospels. In several English translations, the word "amen" on the lips of Jesus has been translated as "verily, verily" or "truly, truly." Several times Jesus began his teaching with the words, "Amen, amen" (John 3:5, 11). What was he saying? The word amen means "so let it be." His message may have been something like this, "Let what I am getting ready to teach you become a reality in your life." "Let it be!"

When the church responds with "amen" it declares, "Thus let it be!" Our prayer response is that the proclaimed word of the gospel become a reality in the world. The "amen" is not reserved for an amen corner in the church but is the solemn participation of the gathered community. Amen is the congregation's word. It is their exclamation mark to the proclaimed word. It is the worshipping community's seal and the signature to their doxology. It is their final shout of praise. It is their hope for the words just prayed to become a reality in the hearts and minds of those who have expressed them.

CHRIST AS THE AMEN

In Revelation 3:14 Jesus himself is called the Amen. "The words of the Amen, the faithful and true witness, the beginning of God's creation." Why? Because Jesus Christ himself is the one who guarantees that our amens will be a reality. We look to him as the source and power to assure us that our prayers will be heard. "Jesus is the embodiment of the truth;" William Barclay observes, "he is the truth. He did not only *say* Amen; he *is* Amen…. To say that Jesus is the Amen is to say that he is the unshakeable affirmation and guarantor of the promises of God."[1]

Helmut Thielicke told the story about a man who experienced a great sense of inner peace and inspired it in others during the dark days of the air raids in Germany. The man shared with Thielicke his

secret. "In the most frightful moments of an air raid, he stopped praying to God and continued only to praise him. That lifted him clean
above the spell of these ghastly moments and, looking beyond these
seconds of mortal terror, he saw the vast expanse of eternity and the
end of the ways of God."[2]

When you and I say, "Amen," we affirm God's presence and
declare, "Thus let it be!" When doxology is on our lips, it is the
church's response that God's kingdom will have its ultimate rule in the
world no matter what evil forces may presently be doing.

As I have wrestled with this great prayer, I have realized the inadequacy of my words to convey the vision of the rich depths of this age-
less prayer. But I know that my life has been edified by my own struggle to understand the truths of this prayer. When you and I read or
pray the Lord's Prayer, I hope that we will always be reminded of the
holiness of the Father to whom it is directed, and the kingdom that
we want to rule our lives. This prayer touches our smallest and greatest needs. From our daily bread, to the forgiveness of our sins, to the
worst evil forces that we will ever meet, we can pray with assurance
that God alone is our deliverer. We praise God for God's endless glory
and power. With doxology on our lips, we shout with praise, "Thine
is the kingdom and the power and the glory for ever. Amen." Amen
and amen!

NOTES

[1] William Barclay, *Jesus As They Saw Him* (New York: Harper & Row,
1962), 377, 379.

[2] Helmut Thielicke, *Our Heavenly Father* (New York: Harper & Row,
1960), 155-156.